I0822959

BEDGEBURY FLORILEGIUM

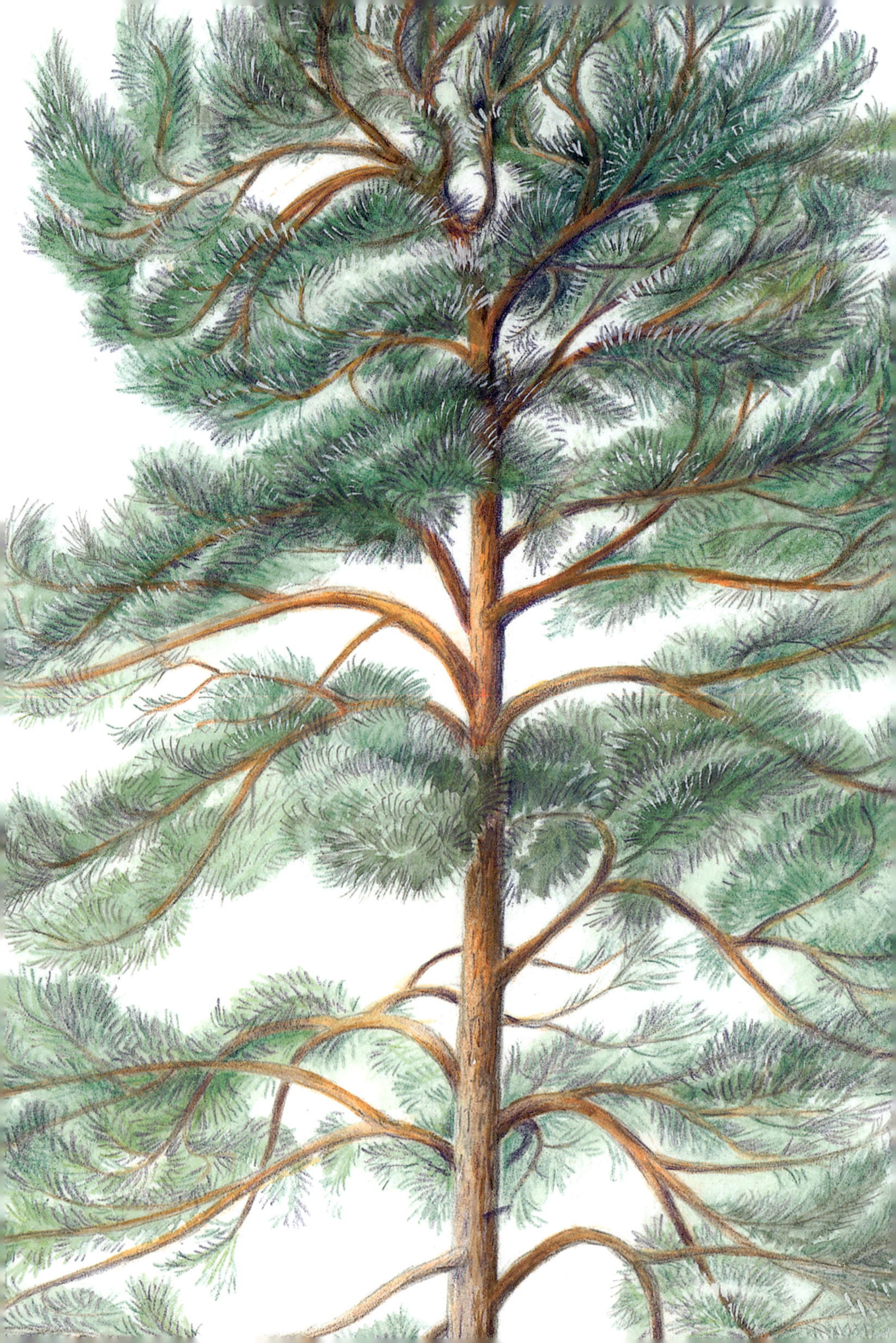

Bedgebury Florilegium

Celebrating 100 years of the Bedgebury National Pinetum

Paintings by
The Bedgebury Pinetum Florilegium Society

Text by
Christina Harrison and Dan Luscombe

Foreword by
Simon Toomer

KEW PUBLISHING
ROYAL BOTANIC GARDENS, KEW

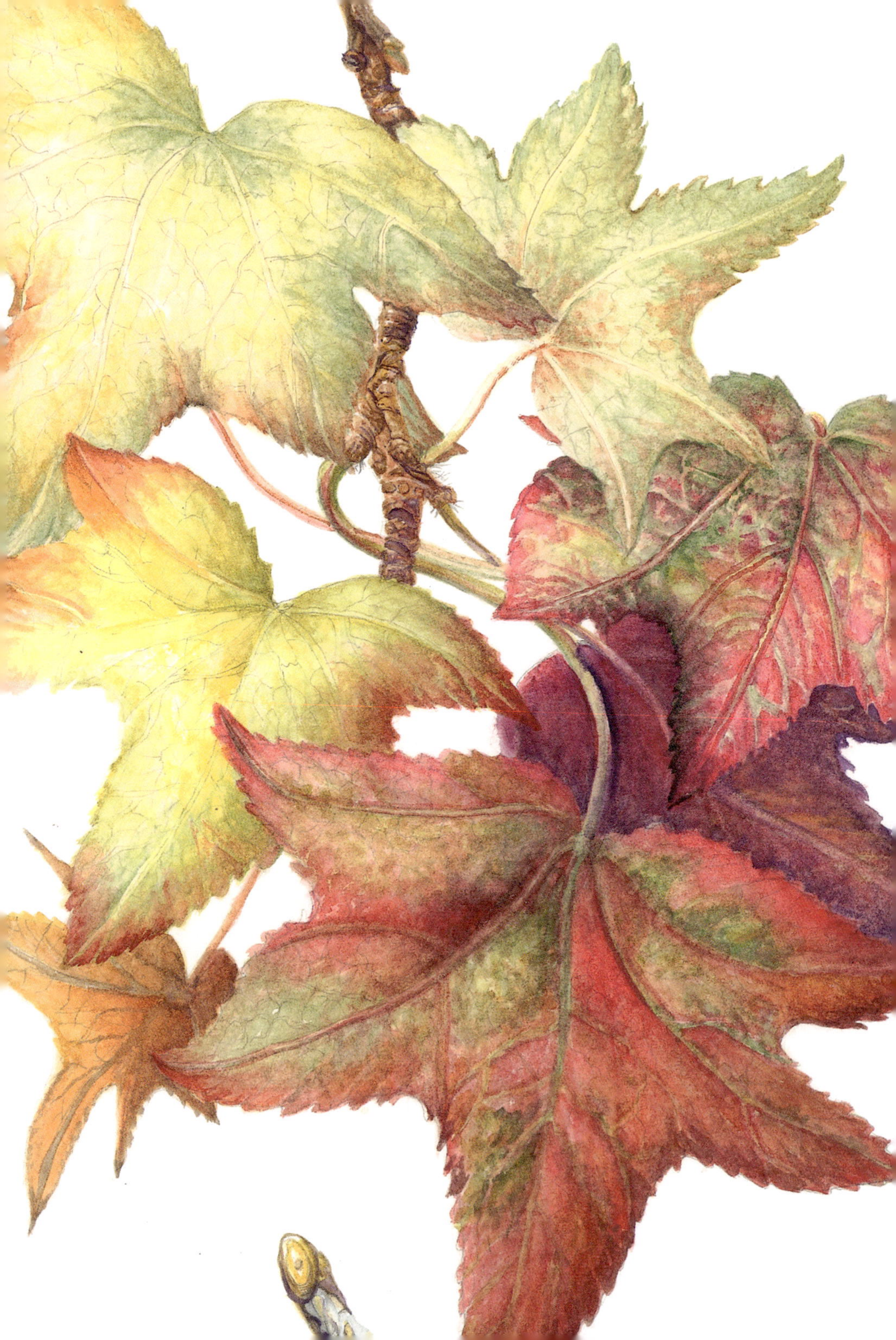

Contents

Foreword

I first visited Bedgebury National Pinetum over 25 years ago and was immediately struck by the variety of both its tree collection and landscape. Like many foresters, my experience of conifers was largely restricted to the small range of species grown in commercial plantations, along with a few ornamentals commonly found in parks and large gardens. Bedgebury soon opened my eyes to the breadth and diversity of the conifer world, and with awareness came a fascination with this amazing group of plants.

The story of Bedgebury Pinetum begins in 1922 when Director of Kew Gardens, Arthur Hill, along with Curator William Bean, sought a countryside refuge for Kew's ailing conifer trees, away from the poisoning smogs of 1920s London. Fortuitously, Bedgebury was offered by the Forestry Commission as a possible location for the proposed new pinetum. Kew botanist William Dallimore was tasked with preparing planting plans and by 1925, planting had begun. The Forestry Commission were keen to support the venture for the opportunity it provided to test new species for forestry.

From this initial collaboration, Bedgebury National Pinetum has become one of the most complete and extensive collections of conifers in the world. As well as a unique living collection for science and conservation, Bedgebury is now a place where visitors can gain a better understanding and appreciation for this often overlooked and sometimes maligned group of plants. Far from the serried ranks of spruce and pine seen in forestry plantations, at Bedgebury conifers can be seen in their full glory as mature specimens set within the beautiful setting of the High Weald of Kent. Over the decades, the strict taxonomic layout advocated by Dallimore has been applied more leniently, with blending of different conifer groups and addition of some broadleaves. This has resulted in a more seasonally interesting and aesthetically engaging landscape for visitors.

Throughout the Pinetum's 100 years, it has risen to the challenges of changing priorities and new threats. From its origin as a refuge and testbed for species to reforest Britain following the First World War, the tree collection is being turned to again to help understand

and select new species to increase climate and disease resilience for our forests of the future. It has also become a refuge at a global scale. With over 30% of the world's 630 or so conifer species listed as threatened, ex-situ collections like Bedgebury's have never been more relevant. The Pinetum has propagated and grown many critically endangered species and distributed them to other collections in the UK and more widely.

In this centenary celebration of Bedgebury National Pinetum, Christina Harrison tells the fascinating story of the people that created it, and those that subsequently shaped it into the place it is today. Running though that story, the illustrations by Bedgebury's own florilegium artists provide a beautiful reminder of the subtle beauty of this wonderful group of plants. The species have been chosen to represent a wide cross-section of Bedgebury's conifers, as well as some broadleaved species such as liquidambar, renowned for its glorious autumn colour.

The book will appeal to readers at any level of knowledge and encourage them to take a closer look at conifers and, I hope, make a visit to Bedgebury to discover it for themselves.

Simon Toomer
Curator of Living Collections
Royal Botanic Gardens, Kew

Bedgebury National Pinetum

The weather on the evenings of 15 and 16 October 1987 caused one of the most significant changes in the Bedgebury National Pinetum since its inception. The Great Storm of 1987 devastated the southeast of England, and Bedgebury did not escape its wrath – nearly a quarter of its trees were lost in a single night. This catastrophe, however devastating, helped shape the future direction of the Pinetum. Space had opened where it previously hadn't existed.

Inspired by their Victorian counterparts, botanic staff across the country began exploring forests worldwide, collecting seeds and specimens to restore and expand their collections. This effort led to the introduction of not only replacement trees but also species that could thrive in the UK's changing climate. Bedgebury became a recipient of some of this new material, and its onsite nursery played a crucial role in growing these specimens.

The team at Bedgebury has followed William Dallimore's principles of growing a wide range of conifers, including both species and cultivars. However, in 2004, a decision was made to move away from taxonomic style of planting. While this method was practical for studying plants, it was proving increasingly difficult to maintain due to the rising prevalence of pests and diseases. The old adage about not putting all your eggs in one basket became evident, especially as climate change led to milder winters, which in the past had helped suppress pests and diseases.

It was remarkably forward-thinking of Dallimore and perhaps a happy accident that moving conifers from climates that didn't suit them into a more favourable environment would become the very heart of Bedgebury's mission. Today, there are approximately 630 species of conifers spread across six continents, yet over a third of them are at risk of extinction in their native habitats. Bedgebury is working with partners worldwide to help ensure the survival of this ancient group of plants.

As part of its support role for the Royal Botanic Garden Edinburgh's International Conifer Conservation Programme, Bedgebury serves as a safe site for hundreds of endangered conifers.

Staff members conduct conservation fieldwork, collecting seeds, studying trees in the wild and sharing skills with conservation organisations on the ground. Seeds collected from these conservation efforts are stored in Kew's Millennium Seed Bank at Wakehurst, used to develop propagation protocols, and grown at Bedgebury's nursery for planting in the Pinetum or distribution to conservation partners worldwide, as well as in trials for species that are more resistant to pests and diseases and those with forestry potential. This work will become even more critical as climate change continues to threaten forest ecosystems globally.

Bedgebury has a horticultural role too! Whether you love them or hate them, conifers are found in almost every garden, and Bedgebury showcases a huge variety of species and cultivars, demonstrating their shapes, colours, and textures. Some, like *Sequoiadendron giganteum* 'Glaucum', grow into towering, narrow spires, while others, such as *Pinus mugo* 'Carsten', bring a ray of golden sunshine to the gardens in winter. Ground-covering varieties, like *Juniperus conferta* 'Schlager', form dense, low-growing mats. Although Bedgebury is a pinetum, it has always included a range of non-coniferous broadleaf trees and shrubs, enhancing the landscape's beauty with spring flowers, diverse habits, and stunning autumn colours. Today, around one-third of the specimens at Bedgebury are broadleaves.

Founded in 2008, the Bedgebury National Pinetum Florilegium Society is a group of botanical artists dedicated to documenting the Pinetum's remarkable plant collection through scientifically accurate and artistically stunning illustrations. These amazing artists volunteer their time, working closely with the curatorial team, to capture the intricate details and beauty of trees that are often overlooked or, in the case of large conifers, difficult to see up close. The 20 beautiful paintings featured in this book are a celebration of Bedgebury's centenary, showcasing the beauty and grace of these incredible plants and capturing the essence of the Pinetum that Dallimore lovingly created in 1925, and that Forestry England continues to manage for future generations.

Dan Luscombe
Collections Manager
Bedgebury National Pinetum
Forestry England

The history of Bedgebury National Pinetum

Christina Harrison

On 18 May 1922, Kew's director Sir Arthur Hill received a letter from Roy Robinson at the Forestry Commission saying: 'I understand … that you have been considering … finding a site for an arboretum away from Kew, which is unsuitable for many coniferous species. Perhaps we could help in this respect, as we now have estates all over the country and could spare the relatively small area which would be required.'[1]

Robinson was certainly correct in thinking Kew's conifers were suffering due to air pollution from expanding local industries, poor soil and rainfall. Kew's arboretum curator William Jackson Bean complained that any man working in the pinetum at Kew would come away looking like a chimney sweep, so bad was the sooty pollution being accumulated on their bark and foliage. Kew's conifers needed to escape London.

The idea of a new national pinetum had been discussed for some time – to show and test the growth and survival of as wide a variety of conifers as possible. Now, with this offer from Robinson and Sir John Stirling Maxwell of the Forestry Commission, plans took flight for a joint endeavour, and the search was on for the perfect spot to create a new world-class collection that could be used for both research and recreation. Bean visited several suggested sites but soil, climate and the distance from London were key considerations. It was only when Bedgebury – an estate in Kent – was suggested that he began to think the plan would work.

Visiting in December 1923, with Kew conifer expert William Dallimore, Bean said that it would not have been possible to find a better place: 'the soil is excellent, the contours of the grounds admirable' and he was swayed by the fact that so many enormous beautiful conifers were already growing there, including Douglas firs (*Pseudotsuga menziesii*), species of *Tsuga*, *Cupressus*, *Thuja*, yew, juniper, pine, and firs including a 'perfect specimen of *Abies grandis*, 100ft high' all of which would provide the nucleus of a new collection.[2] Planting

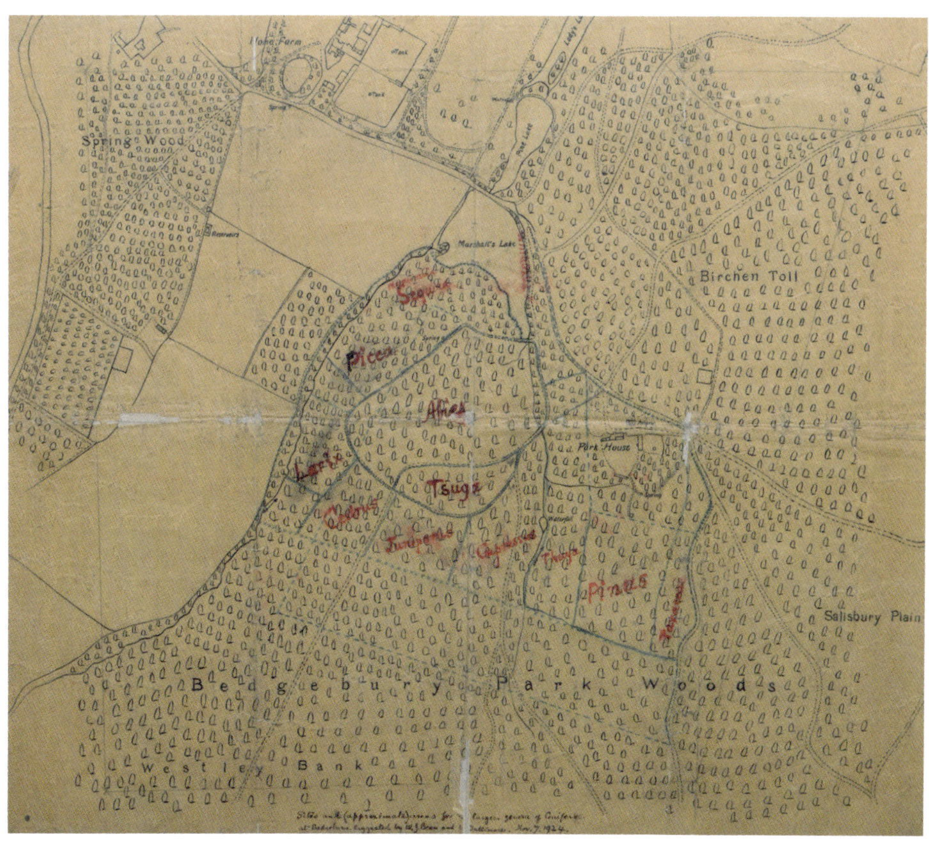

In 1924 Bean and Dallimore drew up an initial planting plan for the arrangement of the trees in the new pinetum.
(B/6/2 RBG Kew Archives)

---

a pinetum among the already existing conifers, oaks and chestnut coppice in the clean air and with a better water supply, was seemingly the perfect choice.

The Manor of Bedgebury is an ancient site, with occupation recorded as far back as 815 CE in a deed belonging to Kenwulf, King of Mercia. It appears to have been a managed forest ever since, used for chestnut and hornbeam coppice as well as oak, ash and birch. In the nineteenth century it was owned by the Beresford family who were responsible for planting many of the exotic conifers

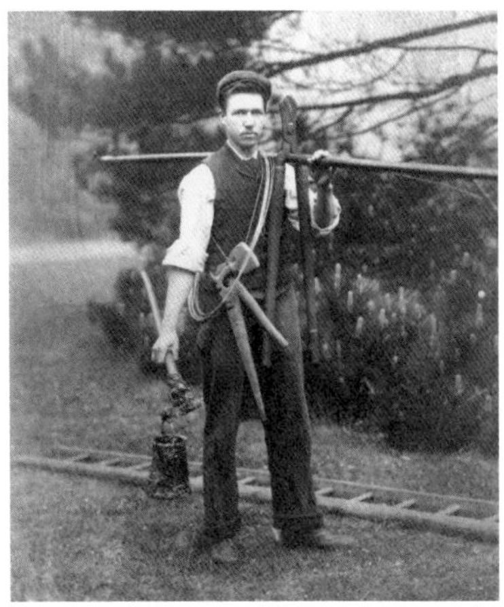

William Dallimore as a young arborist at Kew, before being appointed to help create Bedgebury National Pinetum.

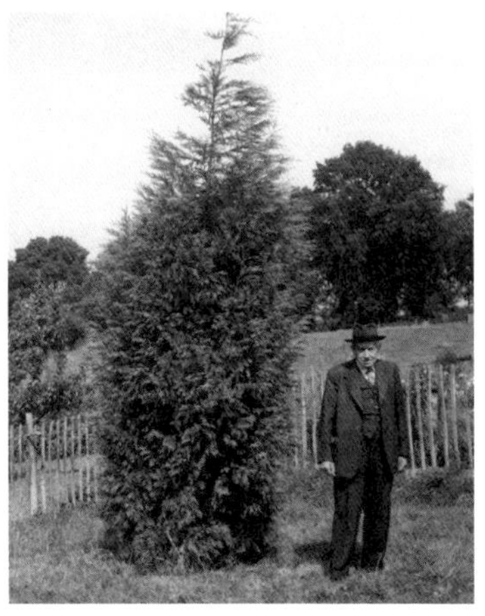

Dallimore, or 'good old Dally' as his former colleagues called him, after his retirement.

near their manor house – including an avenue of Lawson cypress (*Chamaecyparis lawsoniana*) known as Lady Mildred's Carriage Drive. They also created Marshall's Lake as an ornamental water feature. In 1919, the estate was purchased by the government and in 1924 it was transferred to the newly formed Forestry Commission. While Bedgebury forest occupied 2,375 acres, the more ornamented area to the west of the forest, selected to become the new pinetum, consisted of just 50 acres of gently undulating land.

Creating a new pinetum was not a straightforward transition. Hundreds of forestry trees occupying the site had to be felled, including Scots pine, larch, holly, Douglas fir and Sitka spruce. Many of the specimen conifers planted by the Beresfords were kept to help shelter the site. While the Forestry Commission began to clear the land, Bean and Dallimore created a planting plan and a list of around 70 species that could be moved from Kew. They also contacted experts in their botanical network for donations of trees to add to this new national collection. Donors included Gerald Loder of Wakehurst Place and Colonel Balfour of Dawyck gardens in Scotland (now an RBG Edinburgh garden), while other trees were selected for purchase from Hilliers Nursery. By early 1924, many Kew trees had already been moved to a nursery owned by the Forestry Commission nearby.

In March 1925, Dallimore and a gang of Kew workmen made their way down to Bedgebury in great anticipation of starting to plant the new pinetum – a seminal moment in the beginning of a whole new botanical enterprise. However, on arrival, he recorded that piles of timber stood in their way at the entrance. The felling had not been finished and the timber not taken away. 'The only place to unload our young trees was at the foot of the [timber] dump and every one had to be carried over it,' Dallimore recalled, 'many of them were balled up, it was no light task and the work fell upon me. My first job was marking out planting sites. Four men were sent to me from the Forest to dig [planting] holes which were made three feet in diameter and 18 inches deep ... As the holes were dug I carried the plants to their places and helped with the planting. What a tiring job it was.'[3]

'The earliest plantings were species of *Abies*, *Larix*, *Pseudotsuga*, *Cunninghamia*, *Cryptomeria*, *Thuja*, *Tsuga* and *Chamaecyparis*. Whenever possible six specimens of a species and three of a variety were planted,' Dallimore reported.[4] He arranged all the conifers in groups that were related to each other, according to a scientifically arranged plan that also made best use of the soil conditions in different parts of the site. Planting was not a straightforward process as even on the second day they found that rabbits had been undoing their good work and so wire netting had to be placed around each plant to keep them out. This initial planting of 315 conifers in 1925 (including 45 species and varieties of *Abies*, 18 of *Larix*, 13 of *Tsuga*) over eight acres established the Pinetum, but there was much work still to do, including felling trees over another 40 acres.[5] This first planting included 170 conifers from Wakehurst Place and 30 from Dawyck. In February 1926, Dallimore spent an entire month at Bedgebury, planting, fencing and labelling around 1,700 trees, with a Mr Nelmes from the Forestry Commission, while existing trees were also identified, labelled and curated too.[6] New species of *Araucaria*, *Cephalotaxus*, *Cryptomeria*, *Cunninghamia*, and many *Cupressus*, *Juniperus*, *Picea* and *Pinus* (among others) were planted out and diligently recorded. Dallimore and Bean were keen that good records regarding the plants were to be kept (both those that left Kew and any that arrived at Bedgebury) to add to the scientific and cultural value of the trees, and it is to them that we owe the credit for knowing much about the history of the planting and ground management.[7] 'Each young tree was recorded, with its origin, whether raised at Kew or purchased, date of planting, height, cost ... and was given an index number and recorded ... on a label,' Dallimore recalled.[8]

Over subsequent years, felling of the remaining timber trees continued, creating space for the fledgling Pinetum to expand, but this was not without challenges. Managing the water ditches and lake, paths and bridges took a lot of time for such a small team, variable weather threw storms and severe frosts at the new trees, and a whole variety of pests and diseases also caused damage. Spring frosts in the 1920s and 30s were particularly cruel to the young trees, especially spruces and firs. But, while some species suffered, others grew rapidly. Trees were measured and recorded every five years and Bedgebury soon became a valuable testing ground for new and unusual conifer species. Over time some trees were moved around the site to test better growing conditions for them in this living laboratory.

As well as a steady supply of trees and seeds from Kew for both the Pinetum and neighbouring Forest Plots, other trees and shrubs were donated and bought to create more diversity in the landscape. These included a variety of flowering cherries from the famous cherry expert Collingwood Ingram in 1930, 70 rhododendron species and varieties from the Cornish nursery Gill & Sons, seeds and plants from the Barbier & Co and Rafn & Son nurseries in Europe, and others from the gardens of the Rothschild family as well as those from Sir Stirling-Maxwell's own estate too.[9]

After Bean retired from Kew in 1929, it was Dallimore and his Forestry Commission contemporaries Nelmes and Guillebaud who drove forward the management of the Pinetum. Dallimore continued to curate the collection with regular trips from Kew alongside his full-time job there.[10] He also delighted in taking the Kew horticultural students to visit the new collections each year. Over time, it became clear that a permanent staff member was needed on site to manage the collection, and to prevent trespassing, theft and damage to the trees, as well as to look out for the threat of fire. A forester named Castle started in 1929 and came to live on site in a former estate lodge (now called Park House) in 1933. This house was redesigned with one room made into a library and meeting room for use by other staff. By the 1950s, three to four men worked in the Pinetum full-time. As well as continuing to plant and manage the trees, they added to the beauty of the site with more woodland plants such as foxgloves, bluebells, ladies' smock, ferns and cowslips, and even trialled *Linnea borealis*. They also brought waterlilies from Kew for Marshall's Lake. With limited resources Dallimore resorted to tying these waterlilies to bricks and throwing them into the Lake. Despite such violent beginnings (a far cry from the cosseting they usually received at Kew) they soon

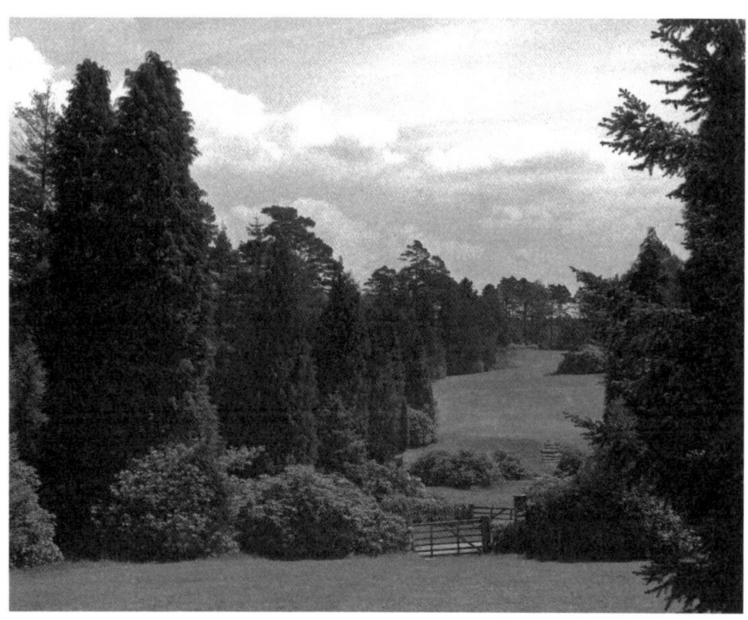

Hill Avenue

thrived.[11] Grassy rides and avenues were also created to add to the picturesque nature of the site, and these became known as Dallimore Avenue and Hill Avenue.

Although severe frosts and some pests and diseases continued to challenge the expertise of the staff, the Pinetum soon began to thrive and it gained a reputation with foresters and visitors alike as *the* place to see new species and varieties of conifer. The collections were expanded over new areas including parts of Home Farm, and Thorn Hill, and here Dallimore moved some of the trees that struggled elsewhere, including the beautiful lacebark pine from China (*Pinus bungeana*). During the Second World War the Pinetum team also began to look after the Forest Plots (a large area dedicated to trialing different timber species) and three women from the Land Army were stationed there to help. Dallimore and Castle described them as 'very capable and hard-working' and were sorry to eventually see them go. Other women were also employed by the Forestry Commission during the war years in the larger forest area nearby. One was to accidentally cause an almost disastrous fire across a wide area by lighting a small

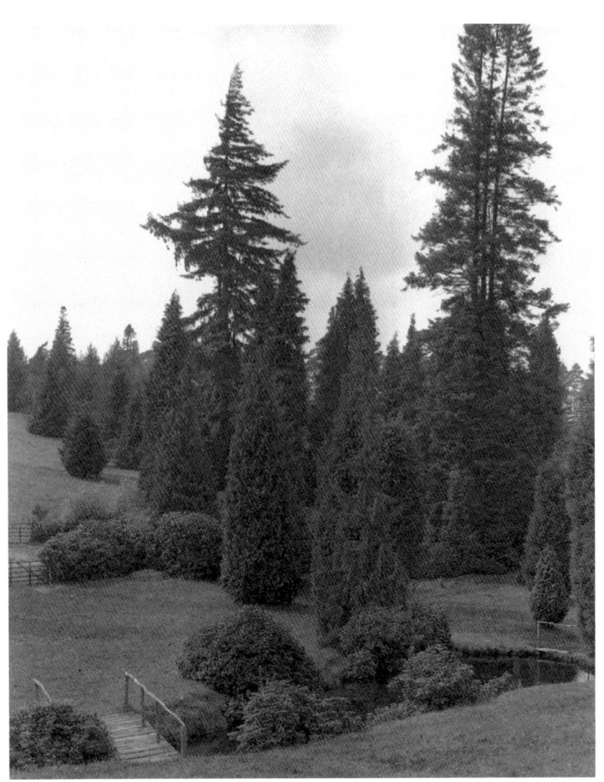

General view across Horseshoe pond

fire to warm her lunch one day. The weather had been warm and dry, and the ground quickly took alight. Despite a large number of firefighters and around 60 soldiers attending the fire, it travelled quickly, destroying 29 of the Forest Plots and drawing ever closer to the Pinetum. It took several days and nights before the fire was finally put out and the Pinetum saved.[12] Other dangers literally fell from the sky during wartime, as the area was not immune to enemy bombs.

Although Dallimore retired from Kew in 1936, he remained an active advisor for another ten years, making weekly visits to Bedgebury.[13] After the Second World War the focus of the governing Committee began to change, and the links with Kew diminished. The new director of Kew, Sir George Taylor took up the offer of starting a new satellite garden and arboretum at Wakehurst Place, building on the exceptional plant collections of Gerald Loder. With the Pinetum established and Kew's focus shifting, the Forestry Commission took over the full management of Bedgebury in 1965.

Dallimore once described a pinetum as needing to contain as full a collection of genera, species and varieties as the climate and soil of the site would allow. It should serve three purposes, he said: to be available for scientific study; to allow anyone interested in trees to view their qualities and make good choices for their own gardens; and to be a testing ground for newly introduced trees for either forestry or horticulture.[14] To his list we can now add perhaps the most important use of all. In the last one hundred years since the establishment of the Pinetum, the need for conservation of tree species has become ever clearer and more urgent. Bedgebury is the perfect place for studying, propagating and growing rare and endangered conifers, working in partnership with other collections around the UK and across the world. The foresight of the Forestry Commission and Kew in establishing this collection will bear important fruit in the decades ahead as climate change brings more tree species to the brink. Bedgebury's trees can offer new hope to those becoming endangered in the wild and offers us the chance to appreciate their sheer beauty and diversity.

---

1 'Bedgebury Pinetum 1924–1934', p.1. RBG Kew Archives

2 Letter from WJ Bean to Arthur Hill, 19 December 1923, 'Bedgebury Arboretum 1922–28', p. 17. RBG Kew Archives; 'Bedgebury Pinetum 1924-34', p. 34. RBG Kew Archives. William Dallimore was assistant curator of the Kew arboretum until 1909 after which he became assistant and then Keeper of the Museums at Kew. He was the recipient of two of the highest horticultural accolades: the Veitch Memorial Medal in 1924 and the Victoria Medal of Honour in 1931.
The Grand Fir, planted by Viscount Marshall Beresford, would become known as the Old Man of Kent and survived until 2016 when it had to be felled due to storm damage and decay. It was 167ft high.

3 William Dallimore. *A Gardener's Reminiscences*. vol. 2. (unpublished, 1951). p. 717. RBG Kew Archives

4 ibid. p. 718

5 'Bedgebury Pinetum 1924-34' pp. 38, 42, and 277–279. RBG Kew Archives

6 Memo from Arthur Hill to Ministry of Agriculture 16 January 1926, 'Bedgebury Arboretum' F18/334 The National Archives; Dallimore, *Reminiscences*. vol. 2. p. 718

7 See: 'Bedgebury Misc Data 1921–1941' two volumes. RBG Kew Archives.

8 Dallimore, *Reminiscences*. vol. 2. p.723

9 'Bedgebury 1924–34' p. 218. RBG Kew Archives; 'Bedgebury Arboretum' F18/334 The National Archives

10 William Dallimore began his career at Kew as a student in 1891, and went on to be a propagator and then foreman in the new arboretum at Kew under William Jackson Bean. In 1926 he became Keeper of the Museums but continued to also manage Bedgebury for Kew until he retired in 1936, after which he remained an honorary curator visiting Bedgebury every week, until 1946.

11 Dallimore. *Reminiscences*. vol. 2. p. 724. RBG Kew Archives.

12 Ibid. pp. 747–749

13 Ibid. p. 738

14 *Guide to the National Pinetum and Forest Plots at Bedgebury*, 2nd edition (HMSO, 1955)

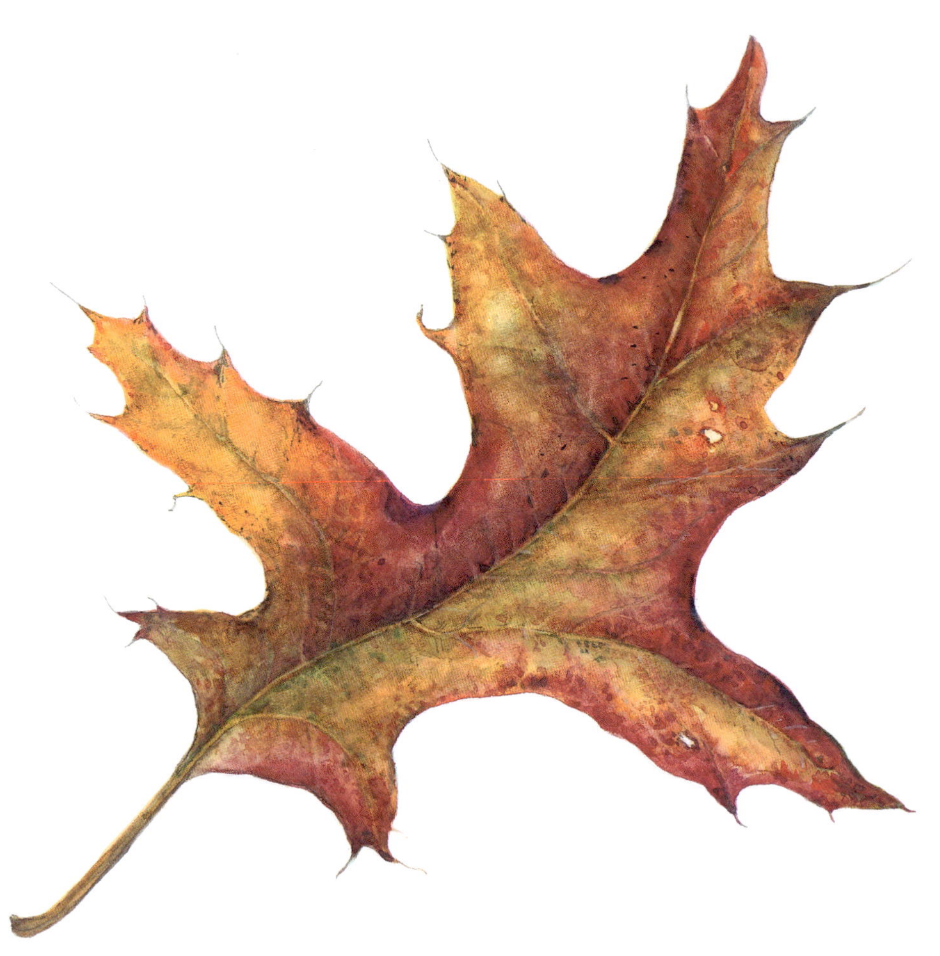

The Florilegium

The Bedgebury Pinetum
Florilegium Society

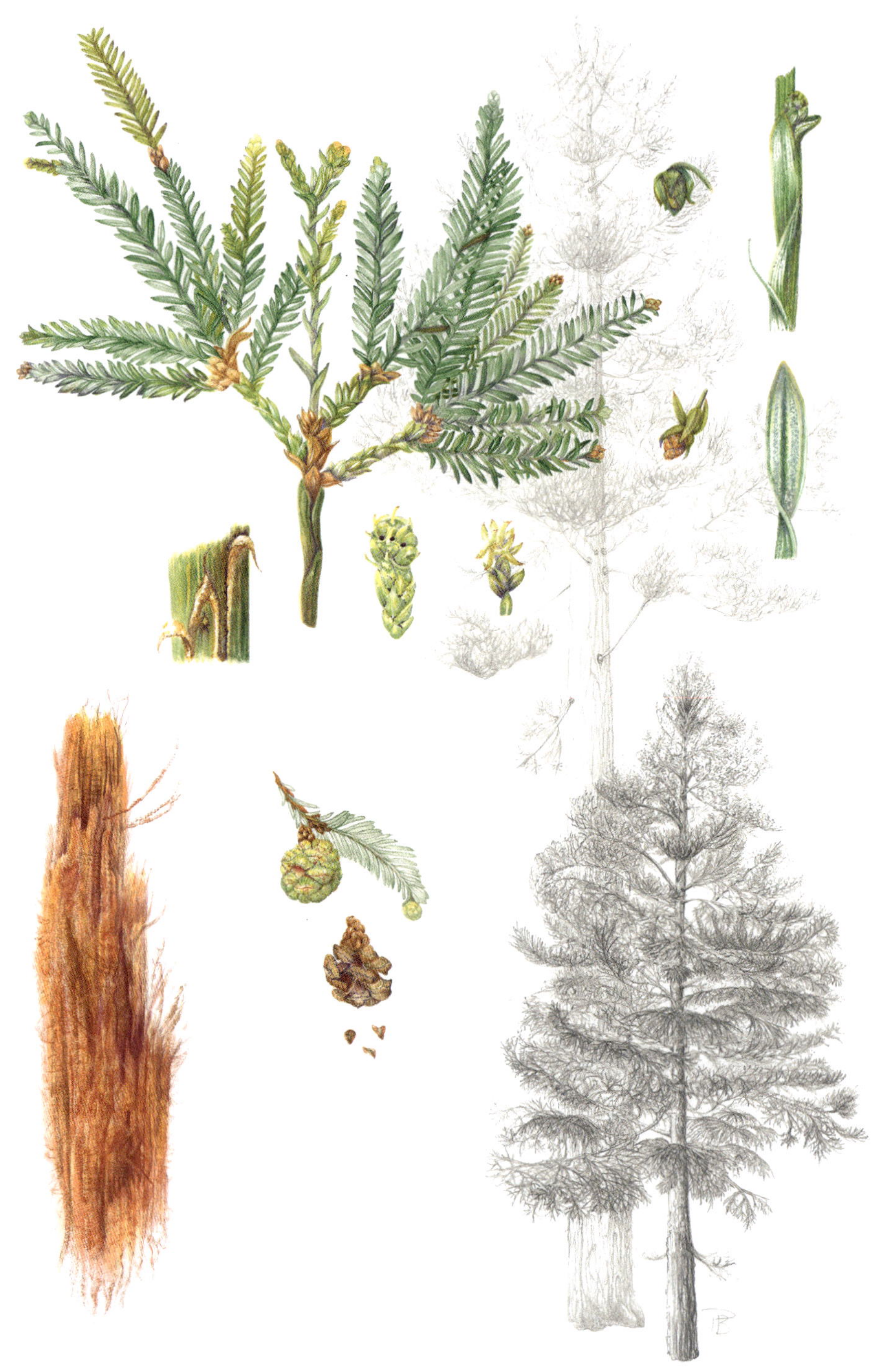

Sequoia sempervirens
Coast redwood
Bedgebury National Pinetum's second tallest tree. In their natural habitat on the USA's west coast these trees live for over 1,000 years and can grow to immense heights.

Pearl Bostock, 2024
Watercolours, graphite and coloured pencils, with white gouache detail

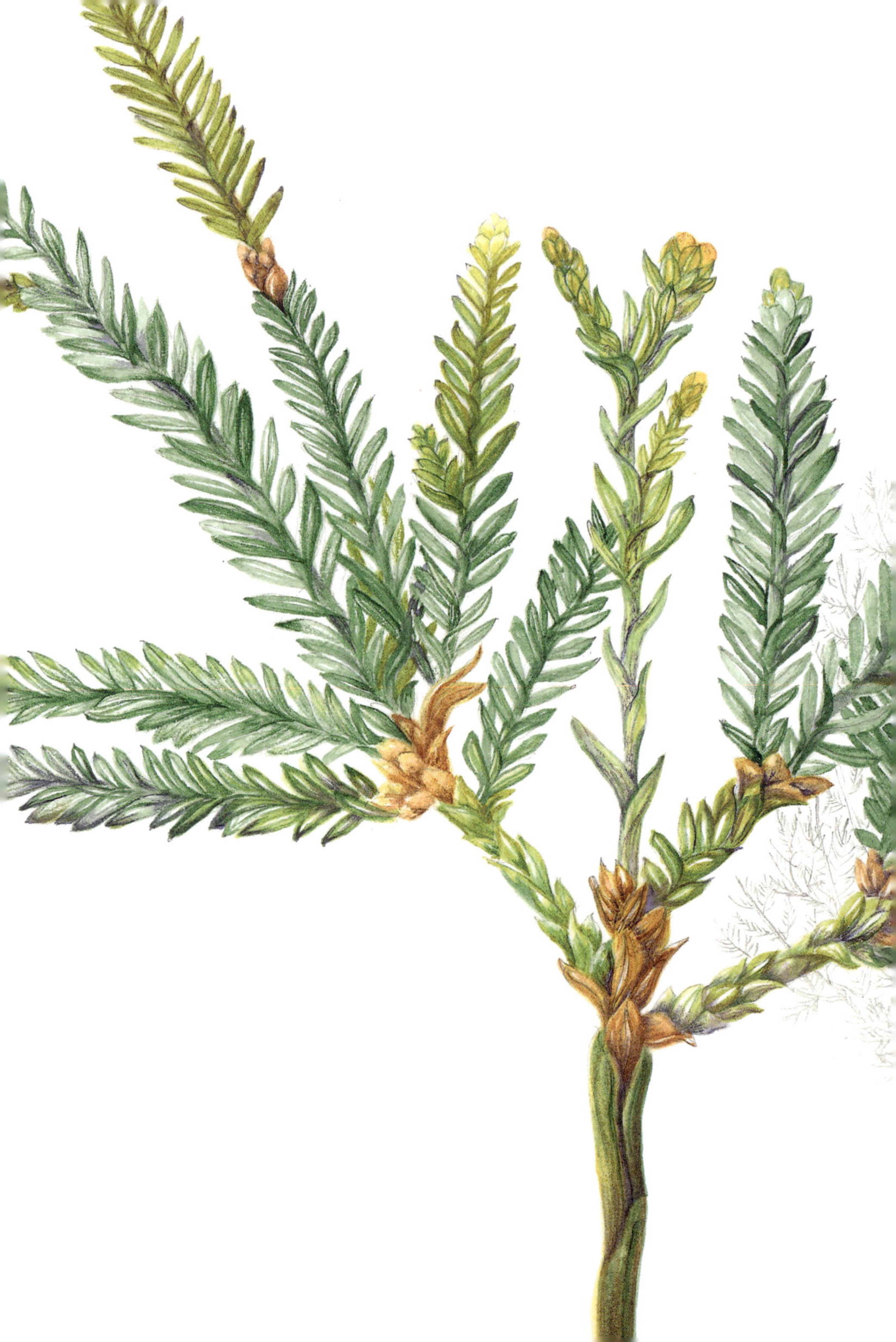

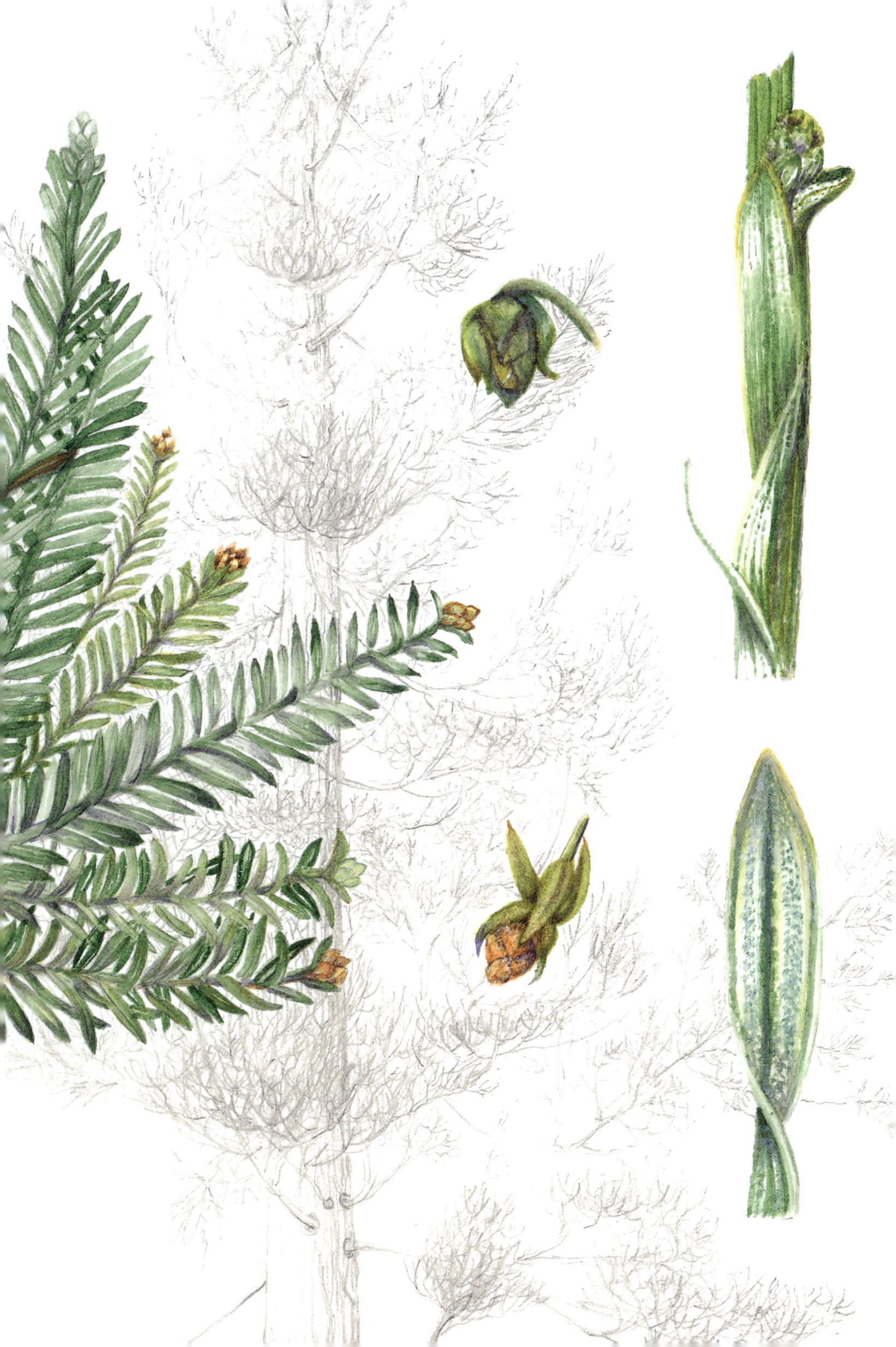

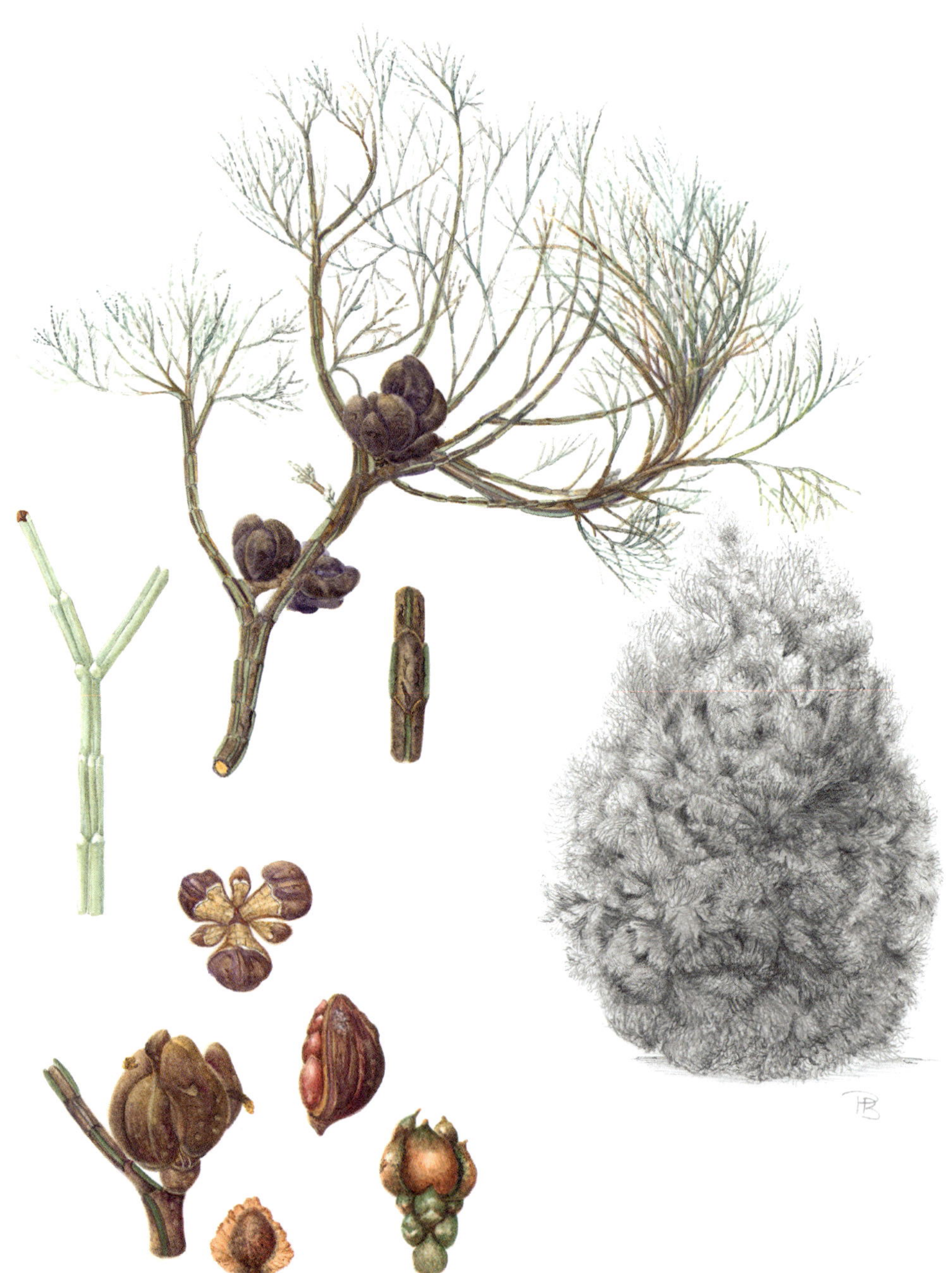

Callitris oblonga
South Esk pine

A threatened conifer from Tasmania and Australia. Only about 3,000 trees remain in the wild due to exotic weeds, feral animals and habitat conversion. Bedgebury National Pinetum staff have collected seeds from across its natural range in Tasmania, for long-term conservation in Kew's Millennium Seed Bank, and for growing in the Pinetum.

Pearl Bostock, 2024
Watercolour and graphite pencil
on watercolour paper

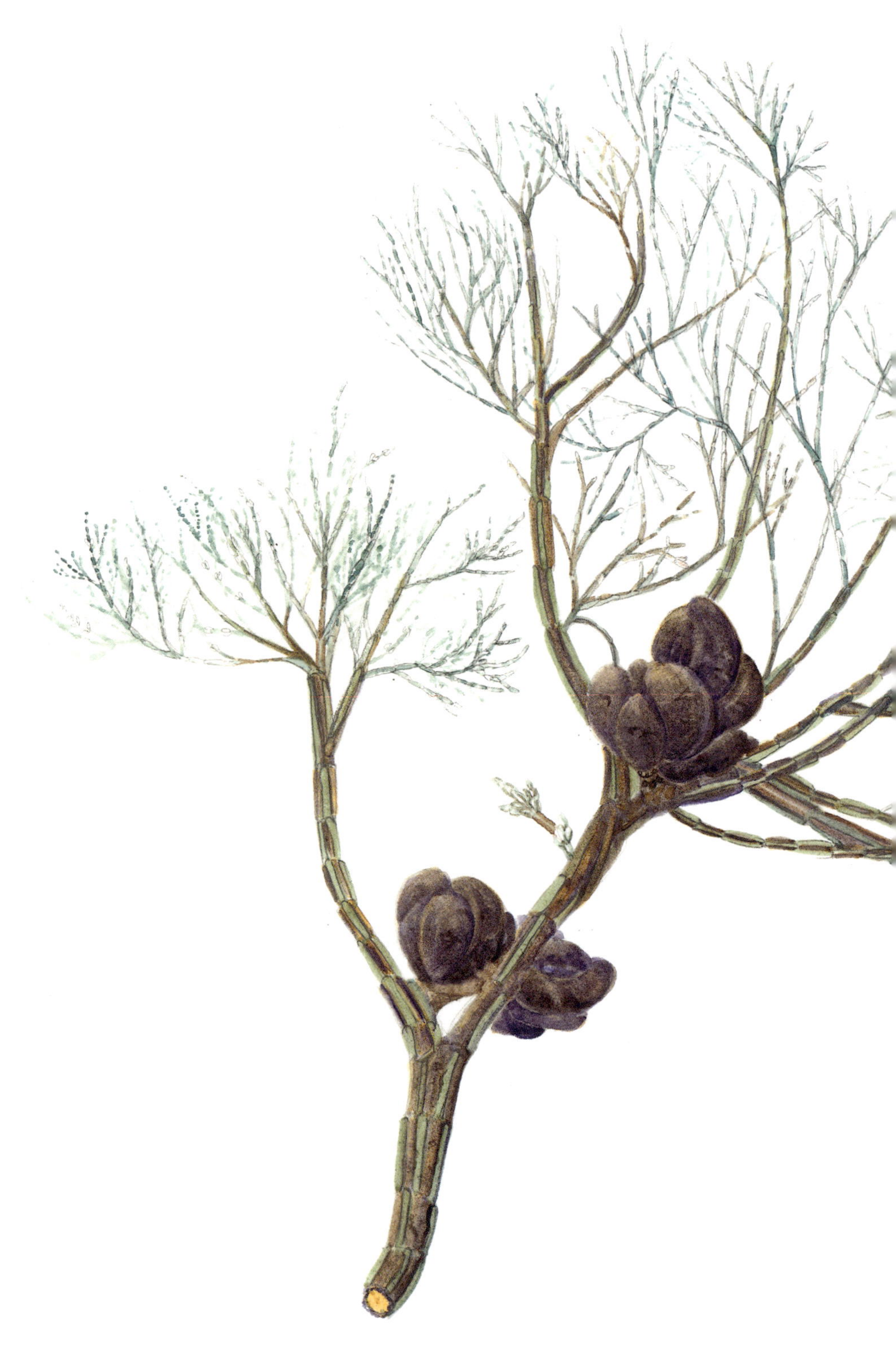

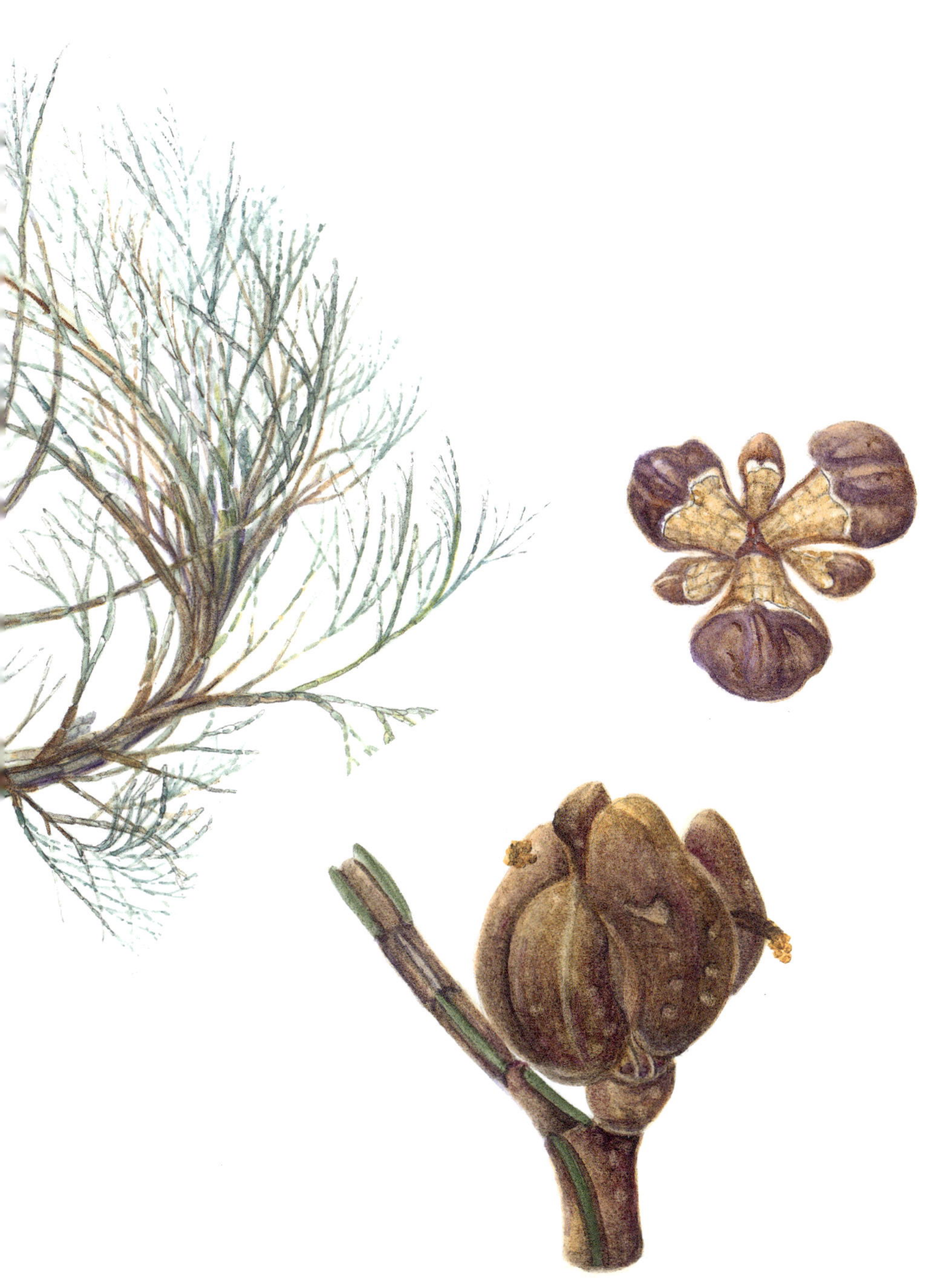

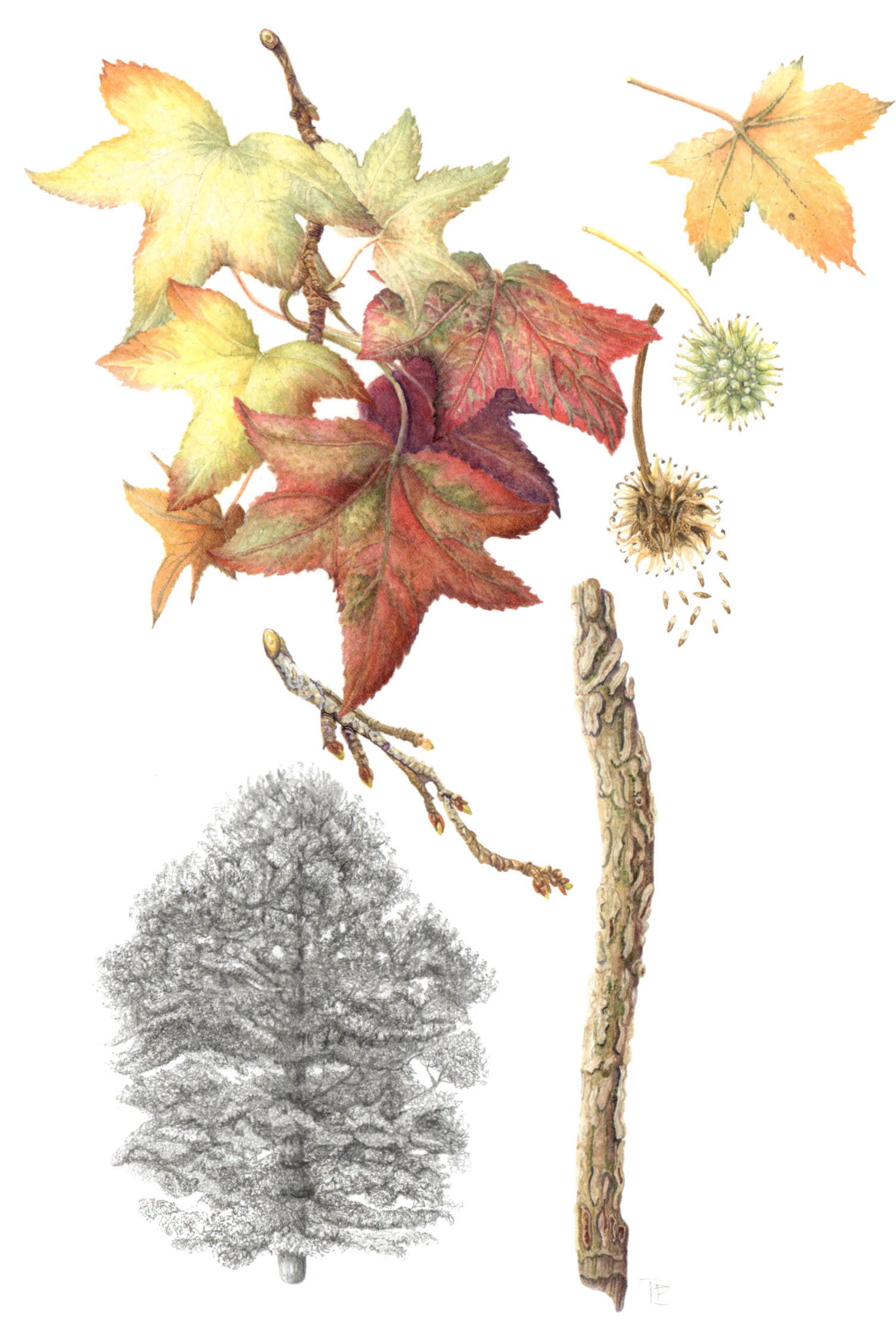

Liquidambar styraciflua
Sweet gum
One of the trees that provides the best autumn colour at Bedgebury National Pinetum. A third of the trees in the Pinetum are broadleaves, providing seasonal interest for visitors.

Pearl Bostock, 2024
Watercolour and graphite pencil on watercolour paper

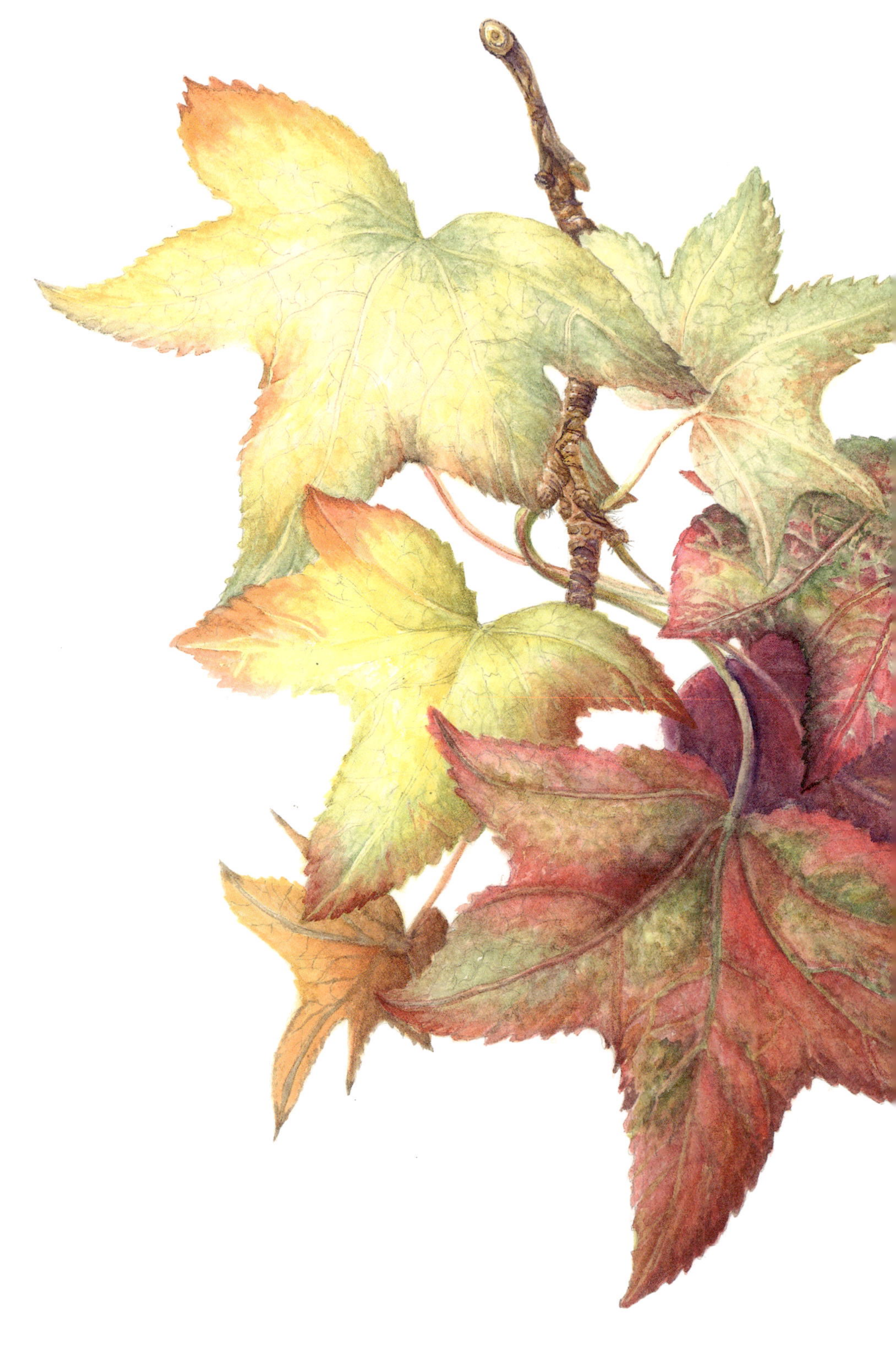

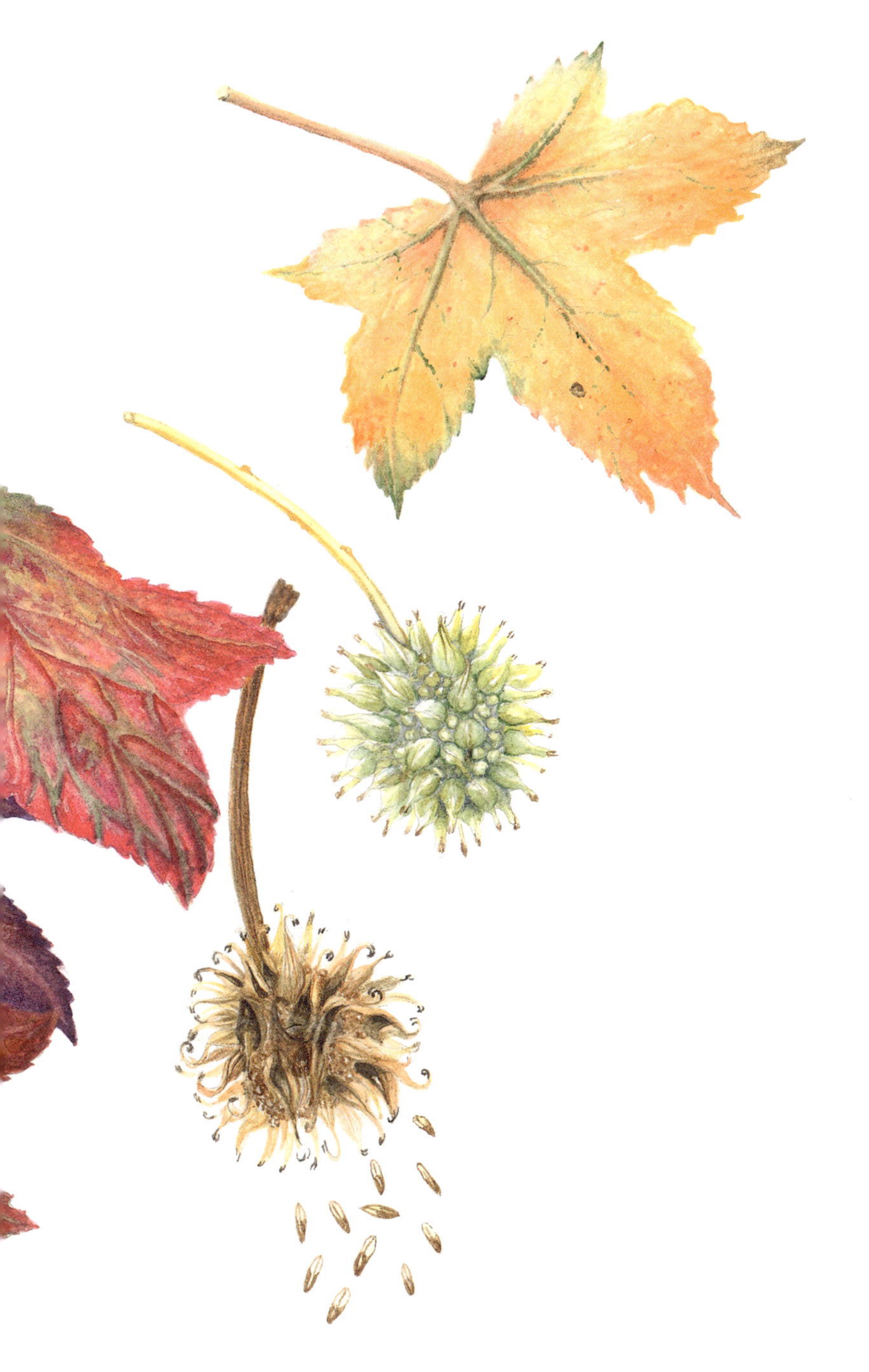

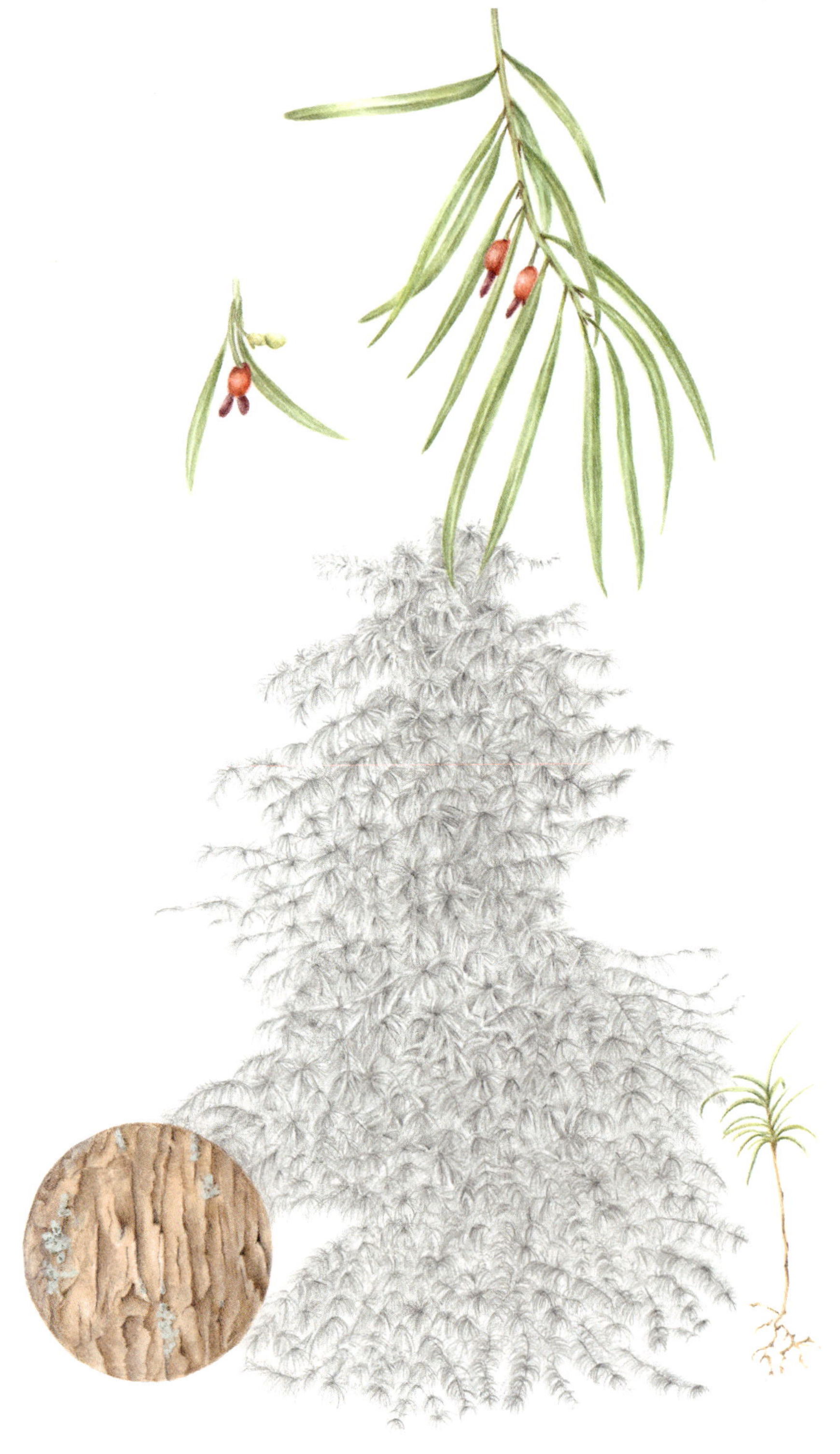

Podocarpus salignus
Willow-leaf podocarp

A beautiful, graceful conifer with 'leaves', threatened by habitat loss in its native Chile. Bedgebury National Pinetum grows these trees as part of its work with the Royal Botanic Garden Edinburgh's International Conifer Conservation Programme.

Julie Spyropoulos, 2024
Watercolour and graphite pencil on watercolour paper

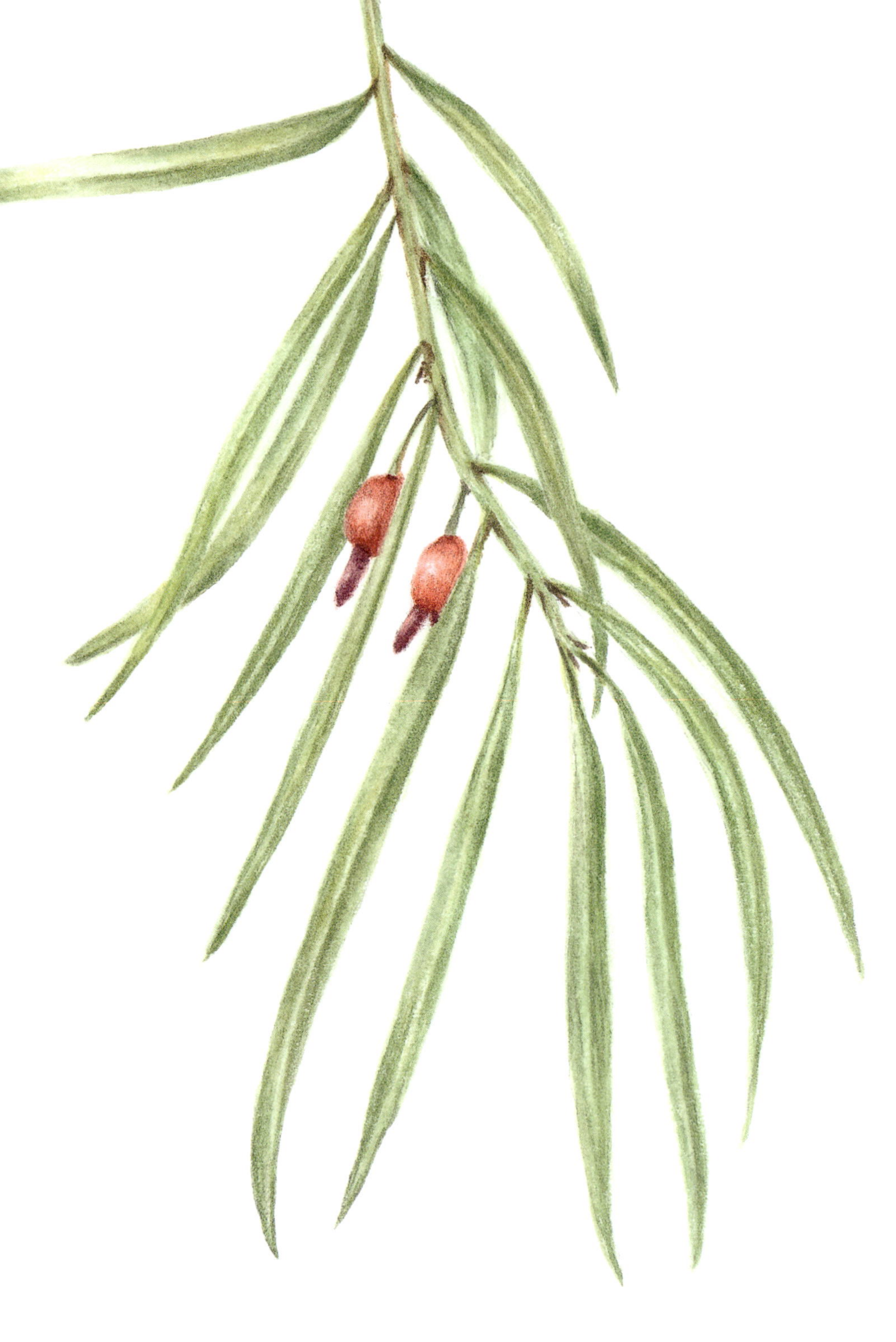

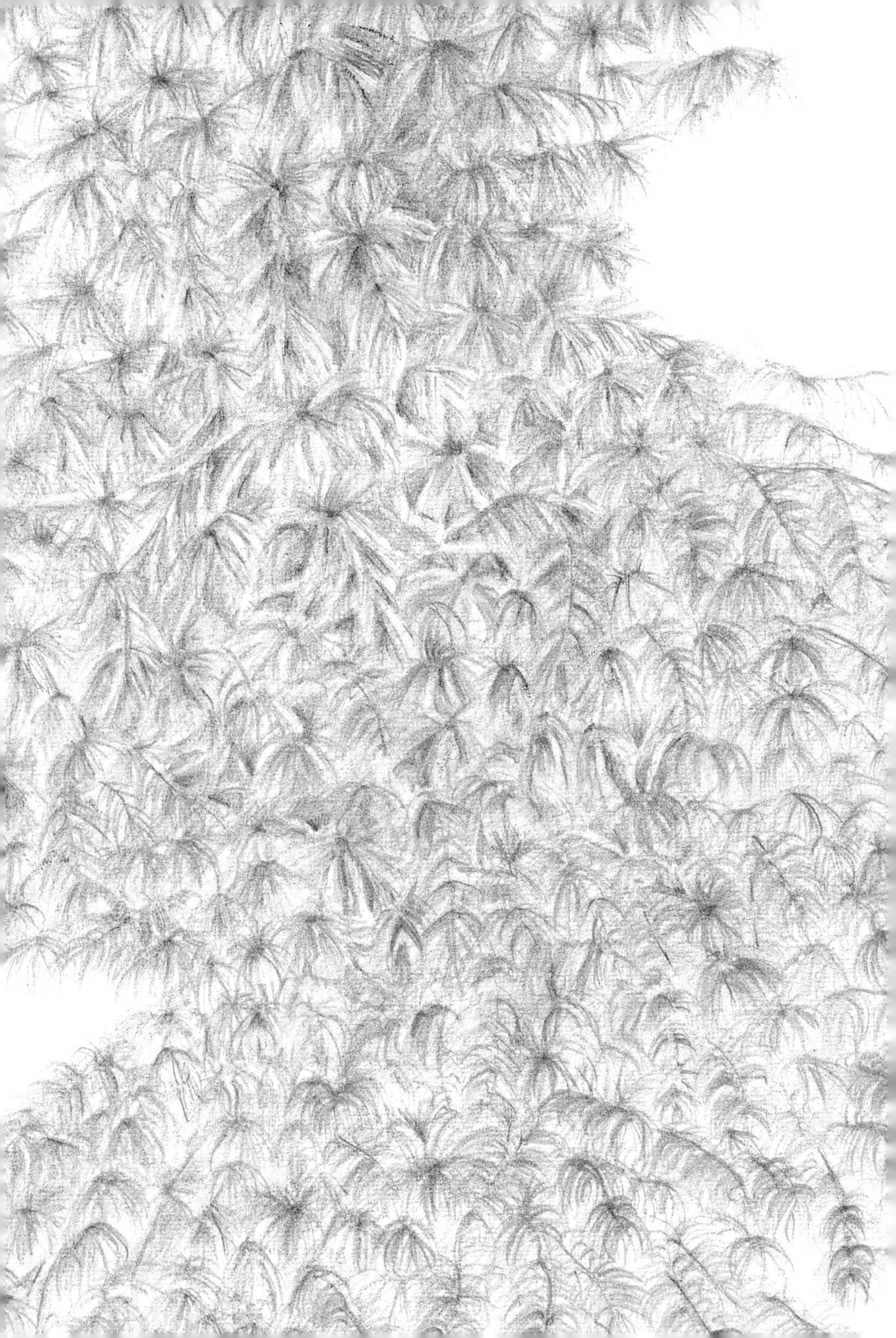

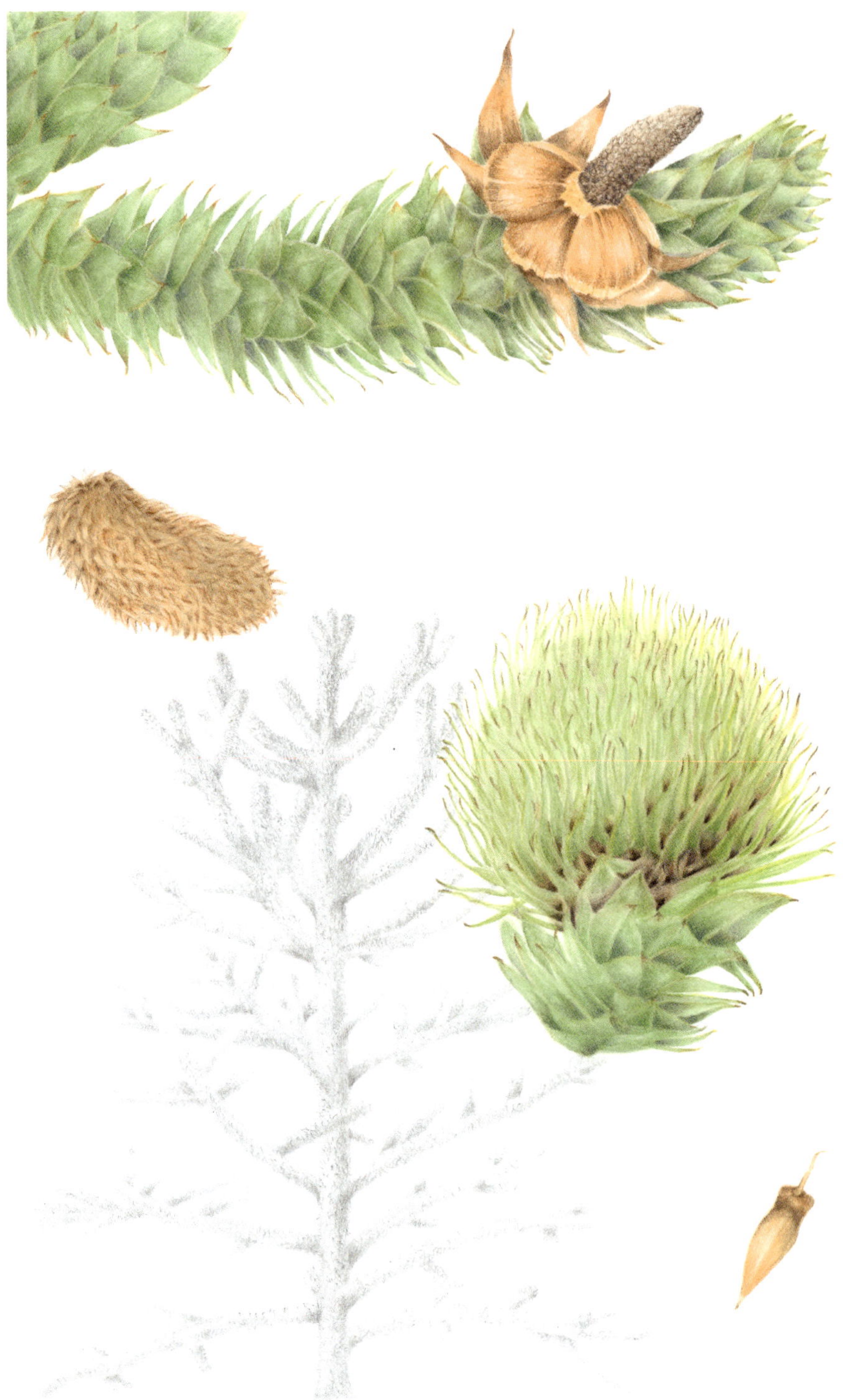

Araucaria araucana
Monkey puzzle

One of the most iconic trees in the British landscape, but highly threatened in Chile and Argentina. The seeds cannot be seed-banked so it needs to be grown in order to conserve it. Bedgebury National Pinetum staff have planted a large area of young trees from seed collected in Chile in 2009.

Julie Spyropoulos, 2024
Watercolour and graphite pencil
on watercolour paper

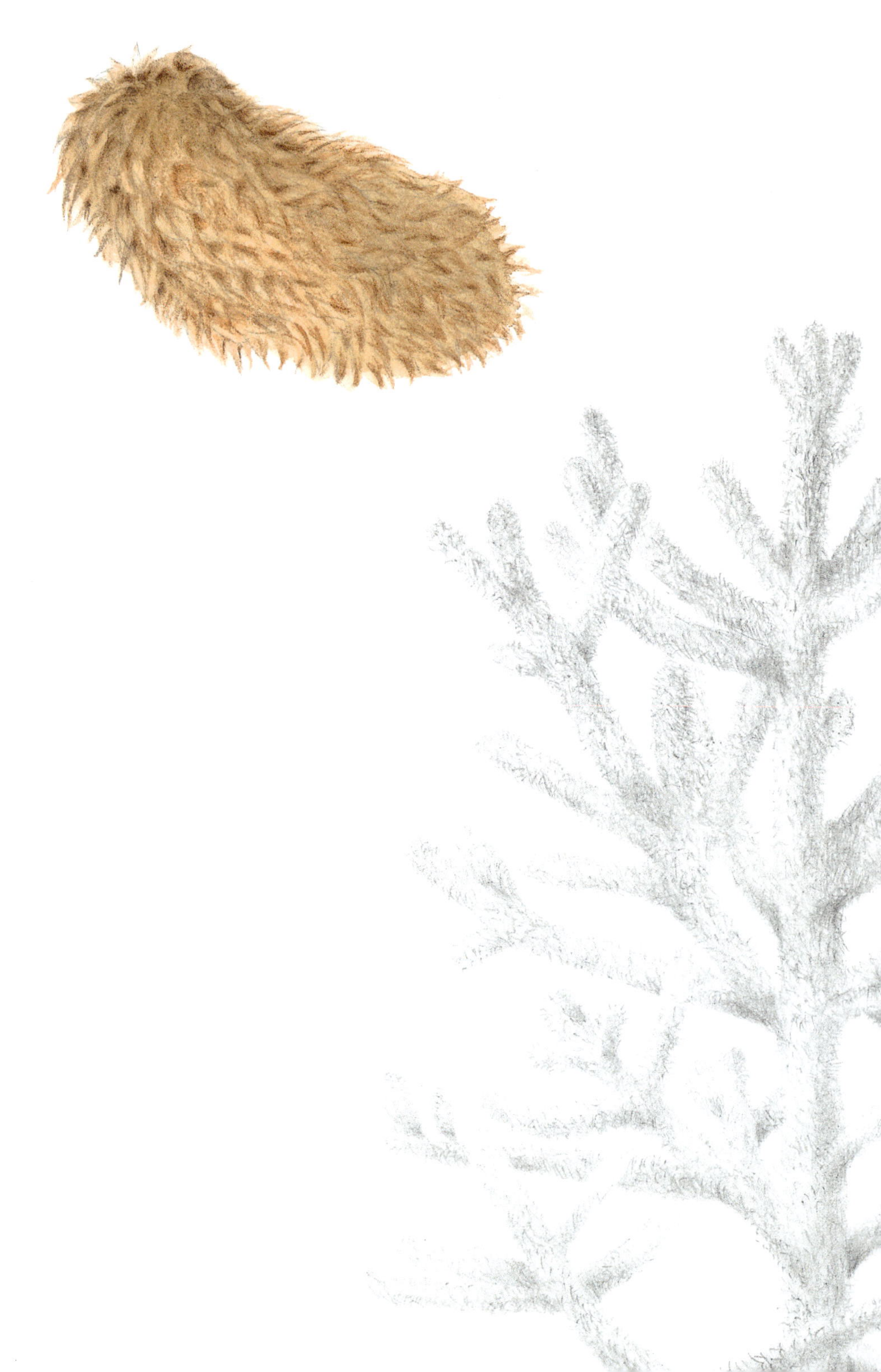

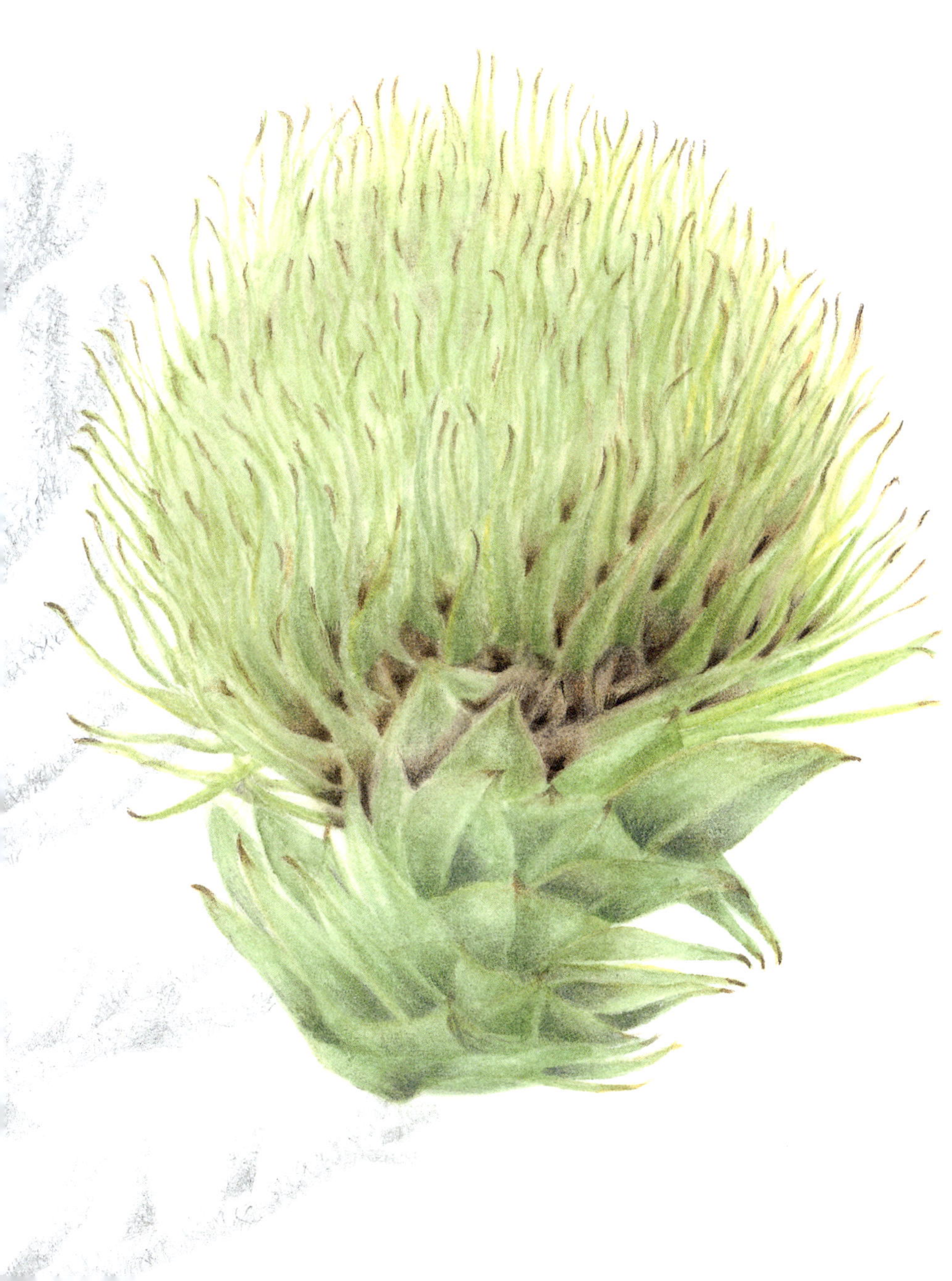

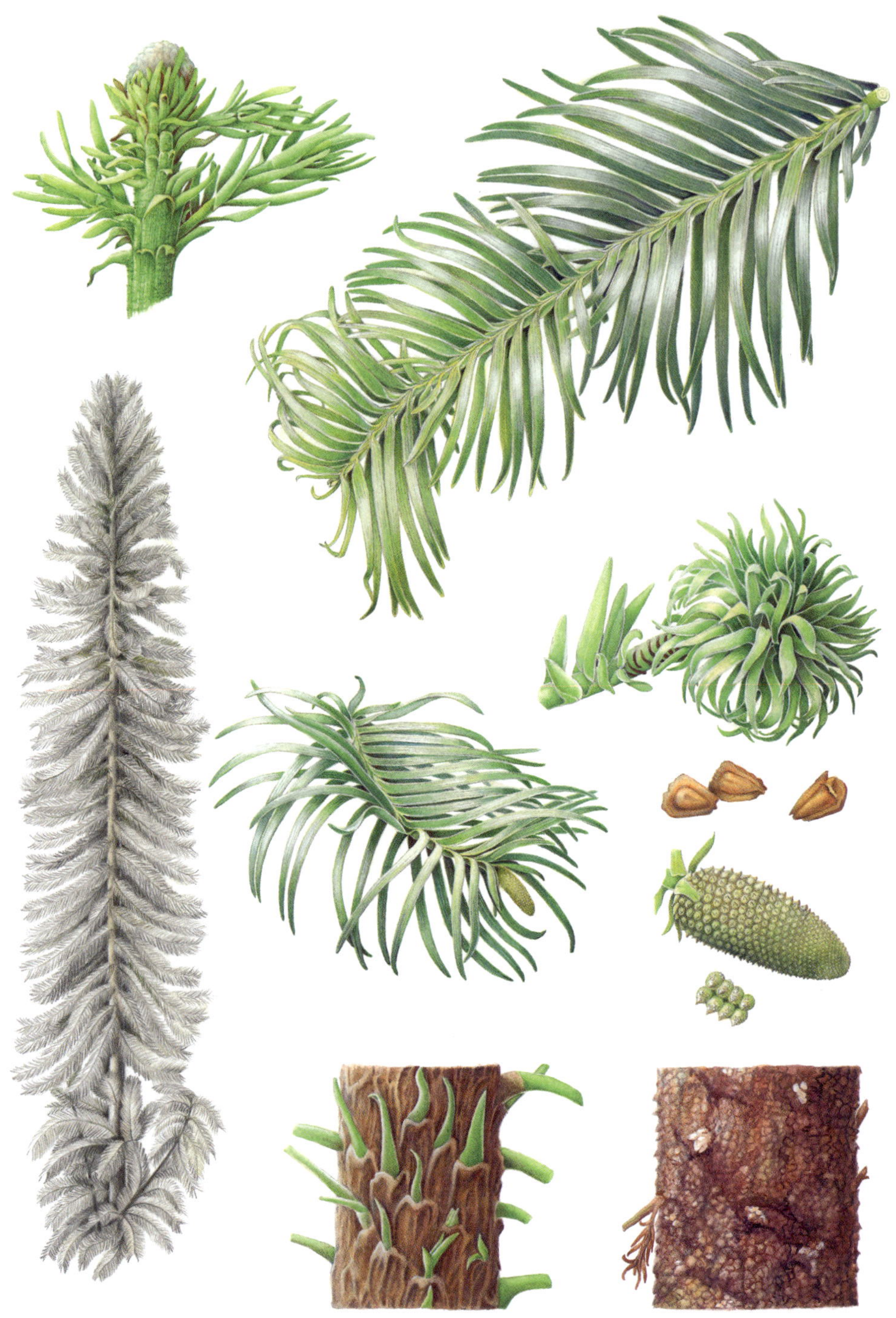

Wollemia nobilis
Wollemi pine
The flagship species of tree conservation. Bedgebury National Pinetum has been involved in an international collaboration with the Royal Botanic Garden Sydney to conserve this tree outside of its natural range, because of threats from climate change in its native Australia.

Margaret Brooker, 2024
Watercolours, graphite and coloured pencils, with white gouache detail

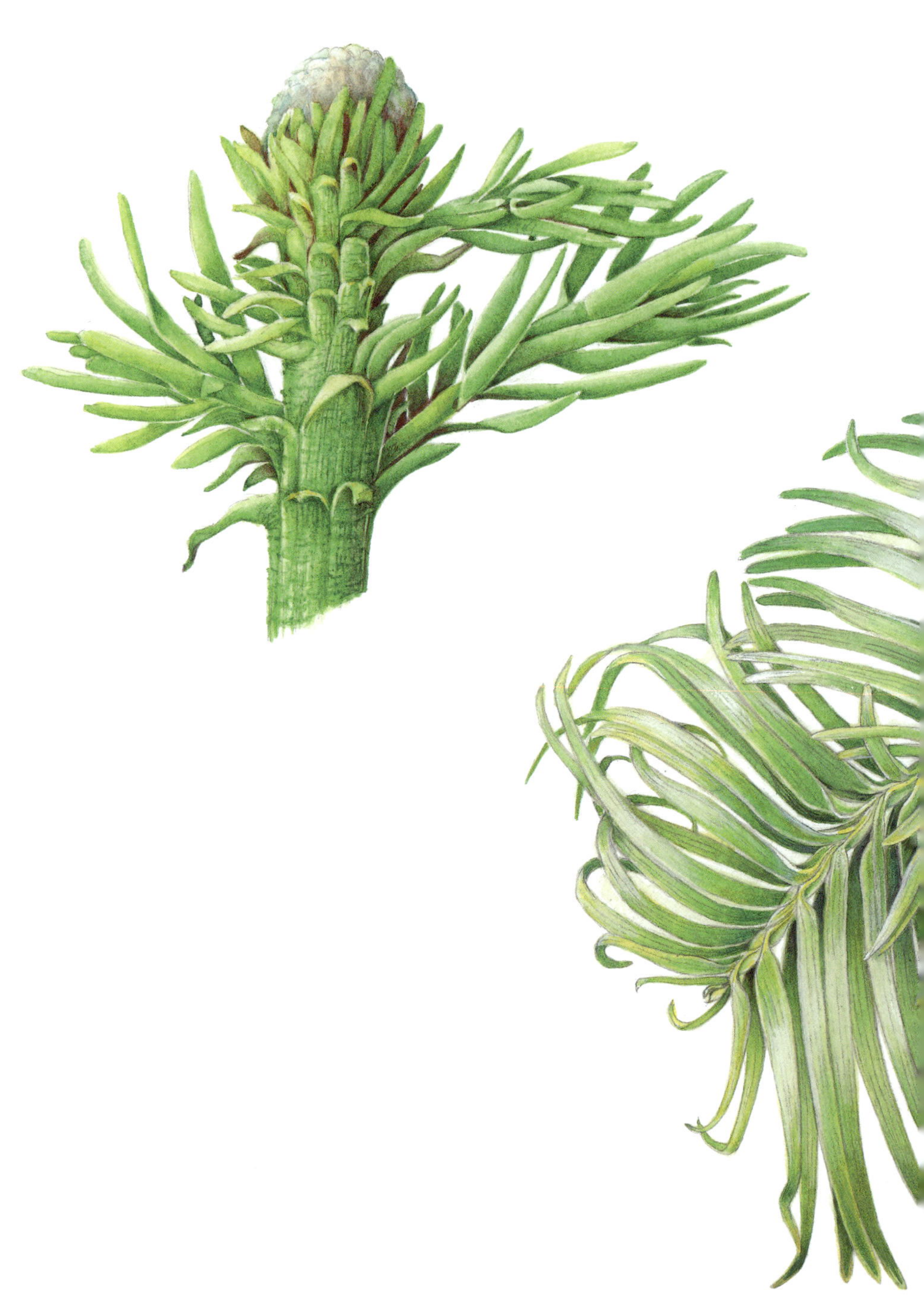

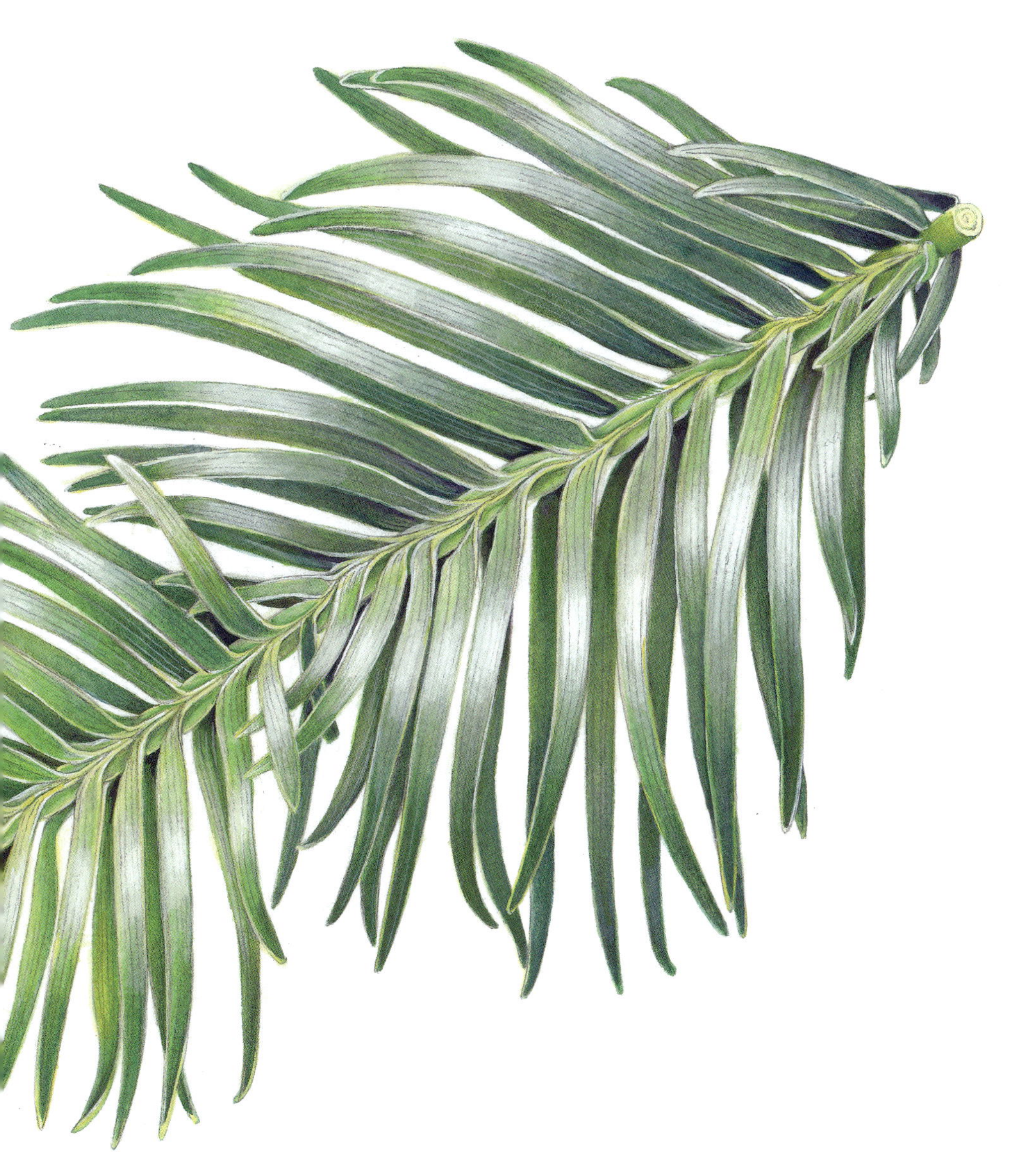

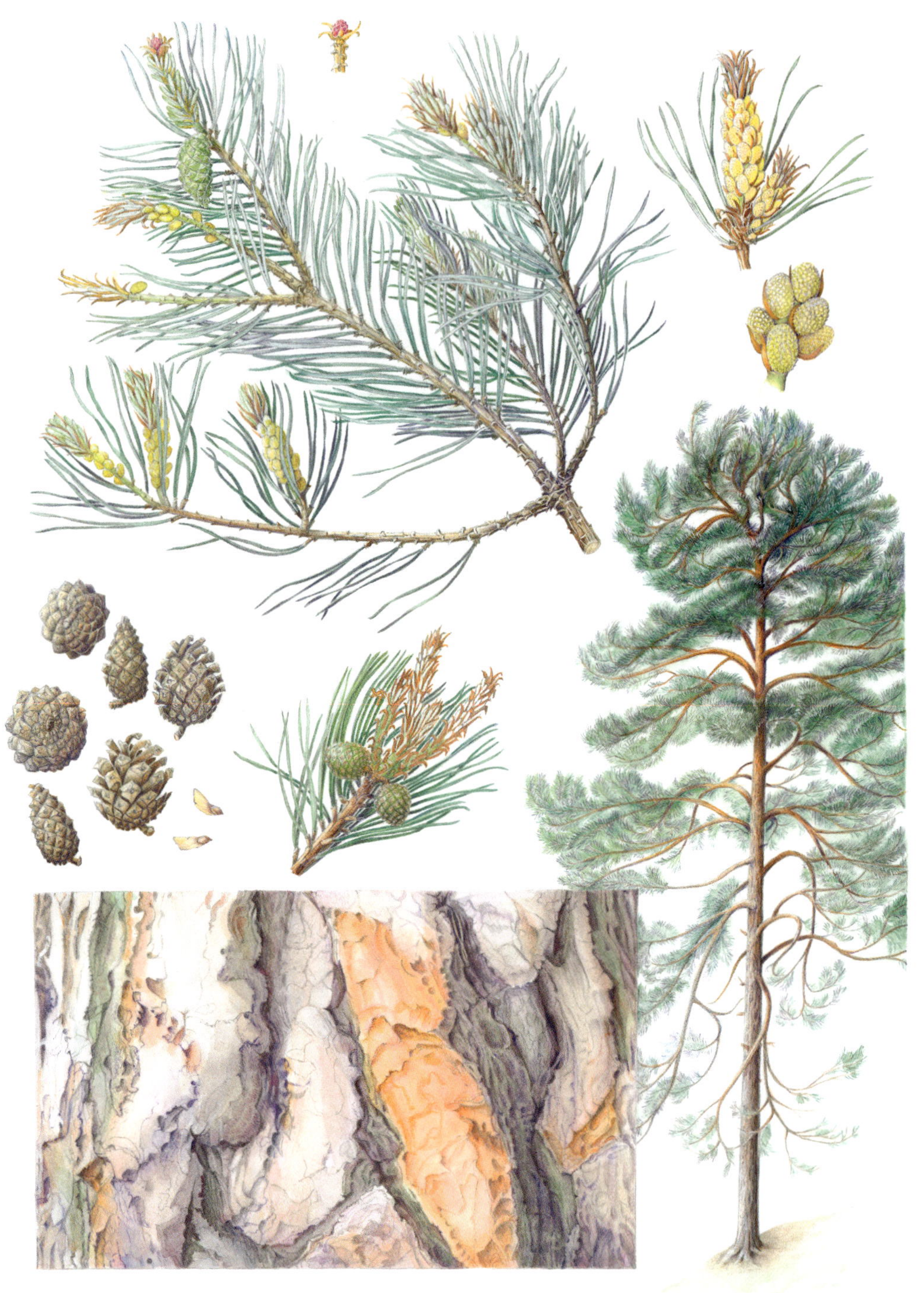

Pinus sylvestris

Scots pine

One of the three British native conifers, the others being juniper and yew. All three can be seen at Bedgebury National Pinetum.

Margaret Brooker, 2024
Watercolours, graphite and coloured pencils, with white gouache detail

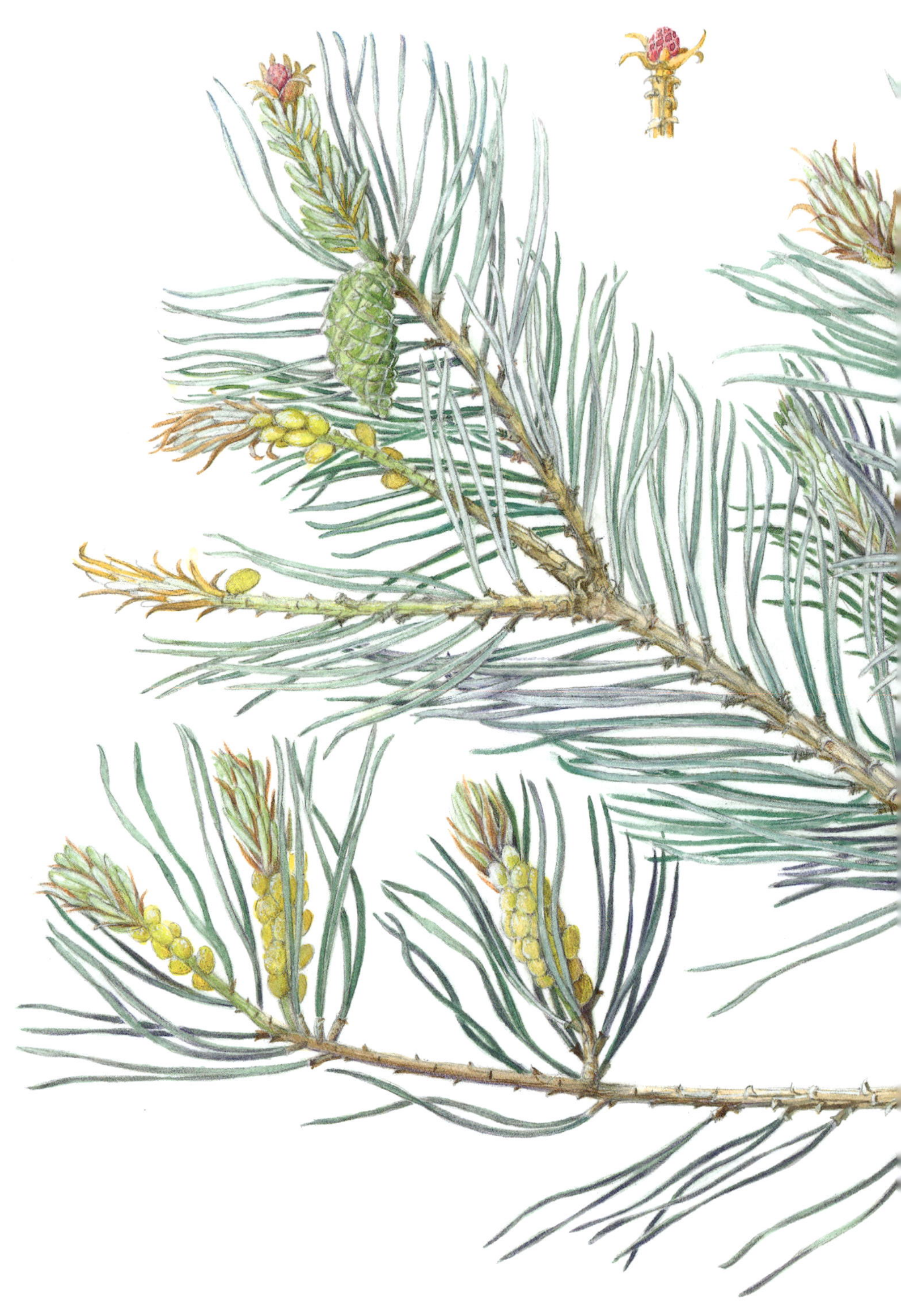

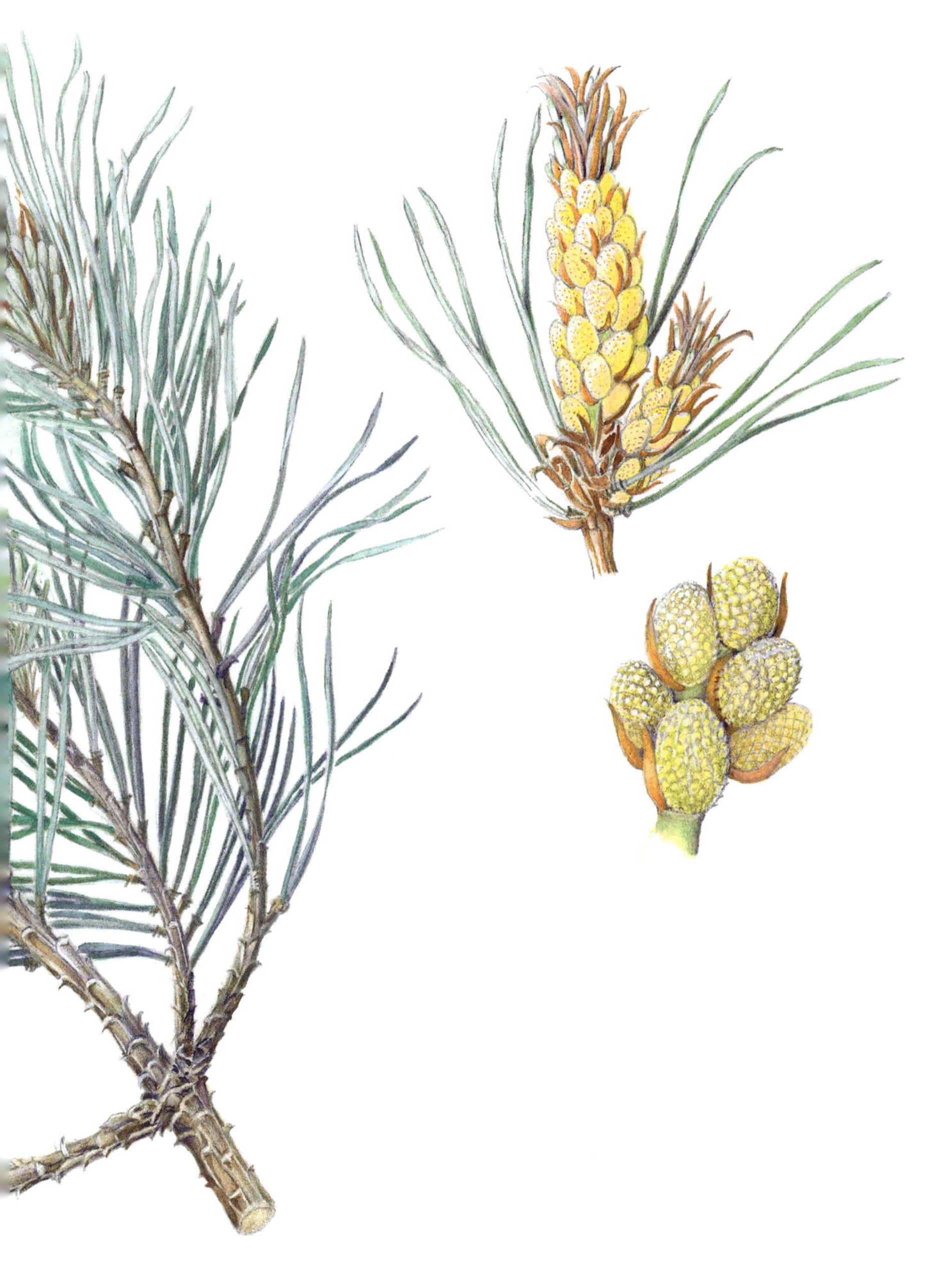

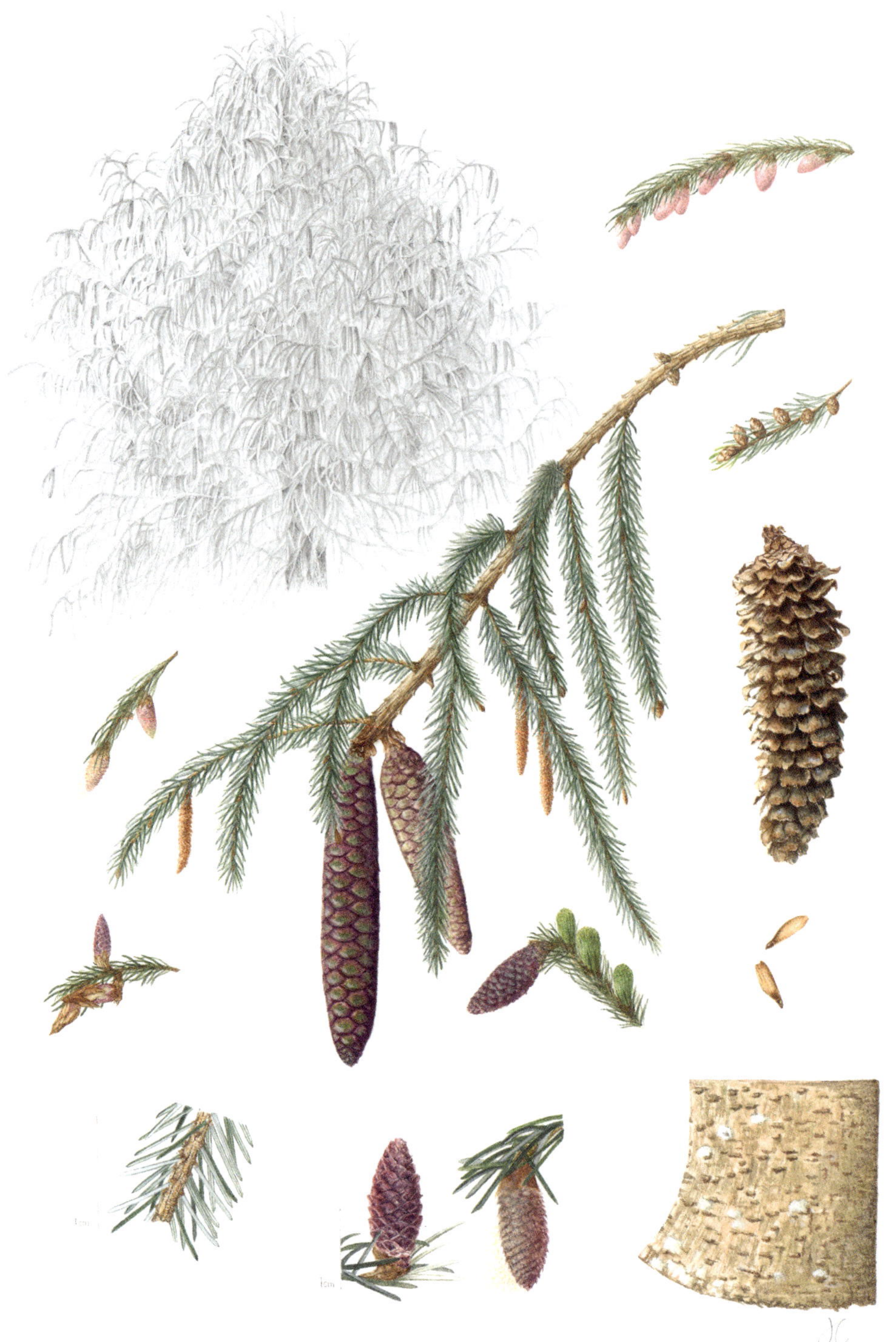

Picea farreri
Burmese spruce

A beautiful spruce with coloured cones that is threatened in the wild. Until recently, all trees in the UK came from the original tree at Exbury Gardens which was lost in the 1987 storm. Bedgebury National Pinetum have re-propagated trees and have given a specimen back to Exbury.

Jackie Copeman, 2024
Watercolour and graphite pencil on watercolour paper

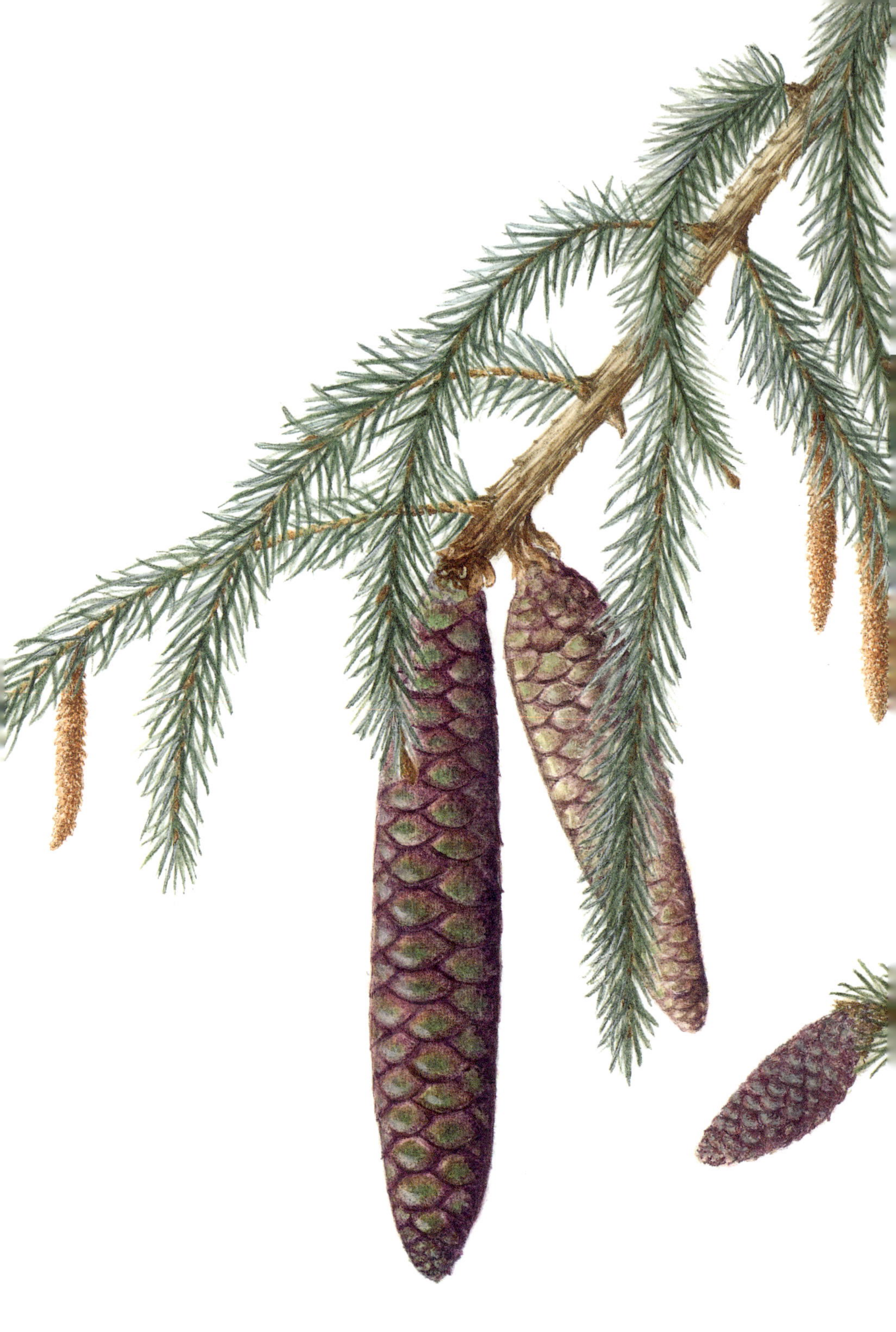

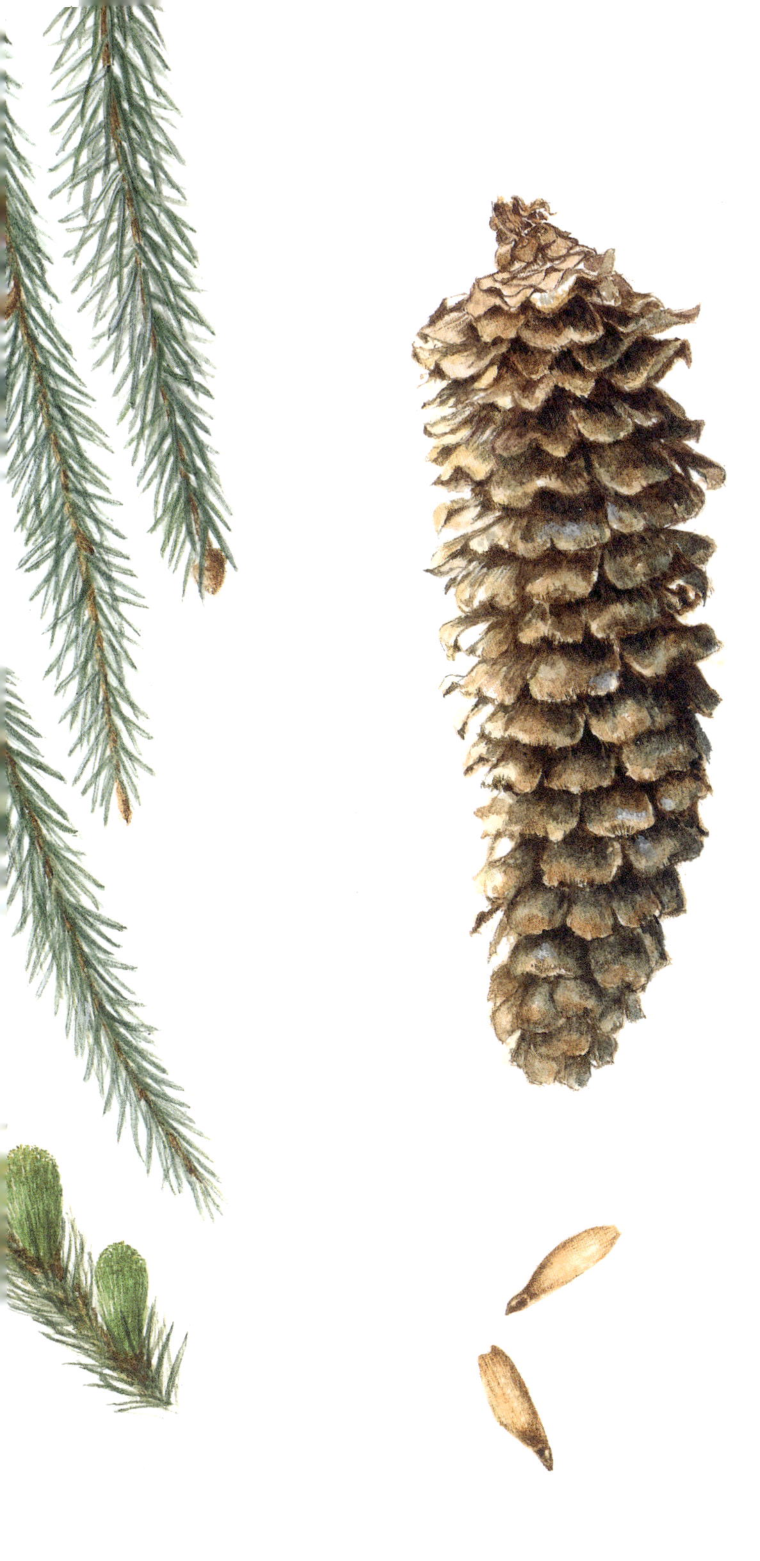

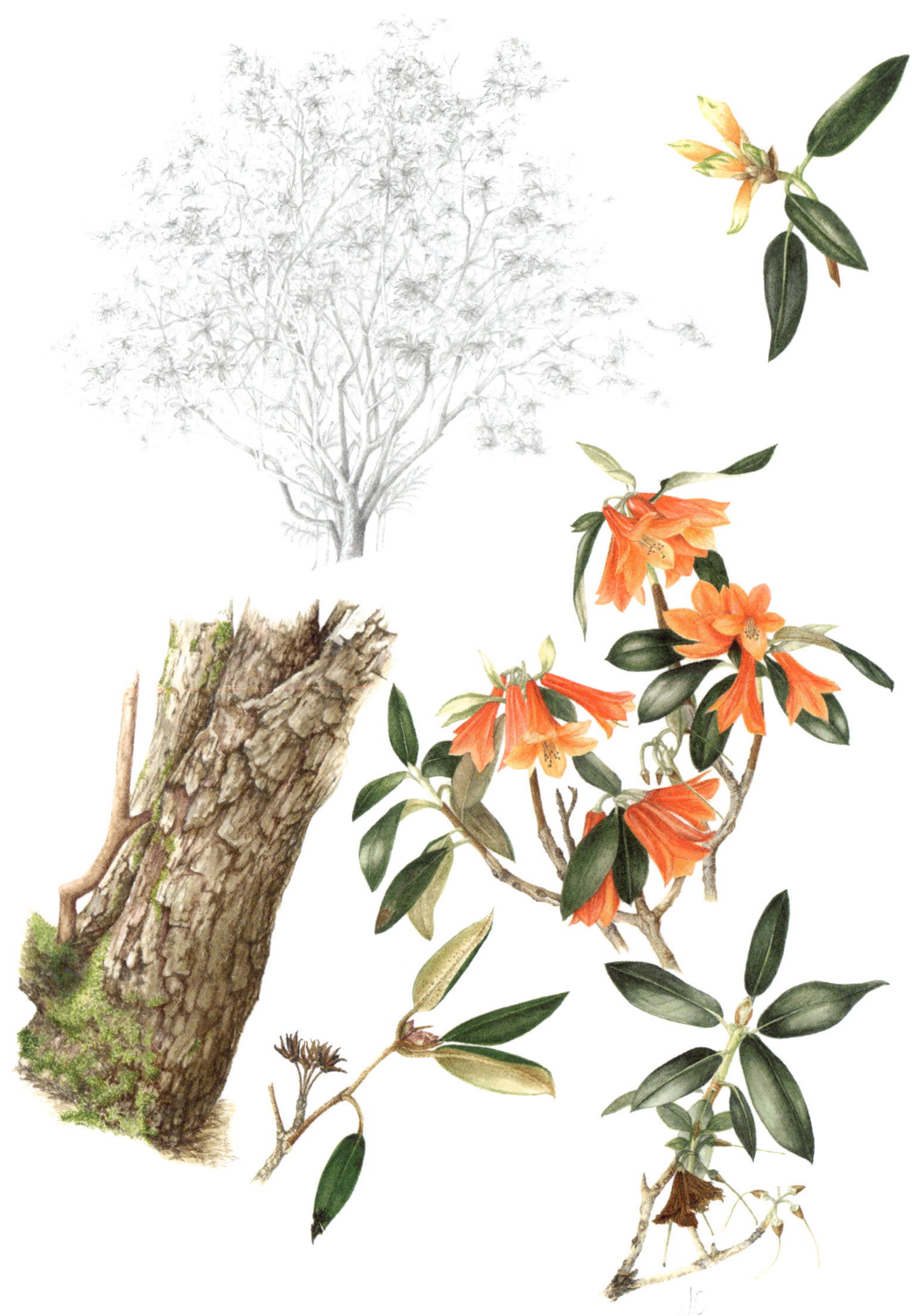

Rhododendron cinnabarinum
Cinnabar rhododendron
Some kinds of rhododendron have gained a bad reputation for being highly invasive. However, many species are highly threatened in their natural habitats. Bedgebury National Pinetum's acid soils make it the perfect safe haven for these attractive plants.

Jackie Copeman, 2024
Watercolour and graphite pencil on watercolour paper

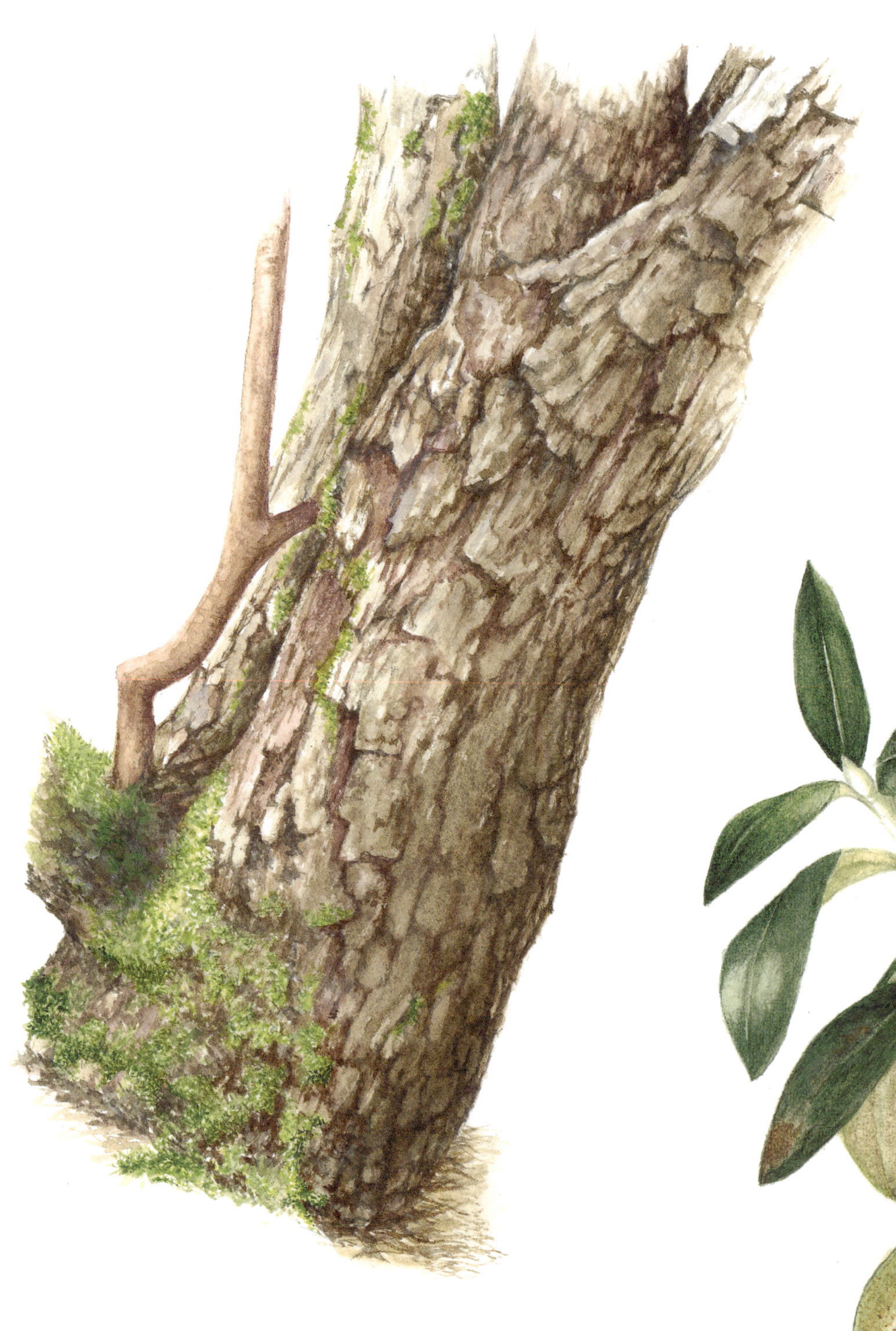

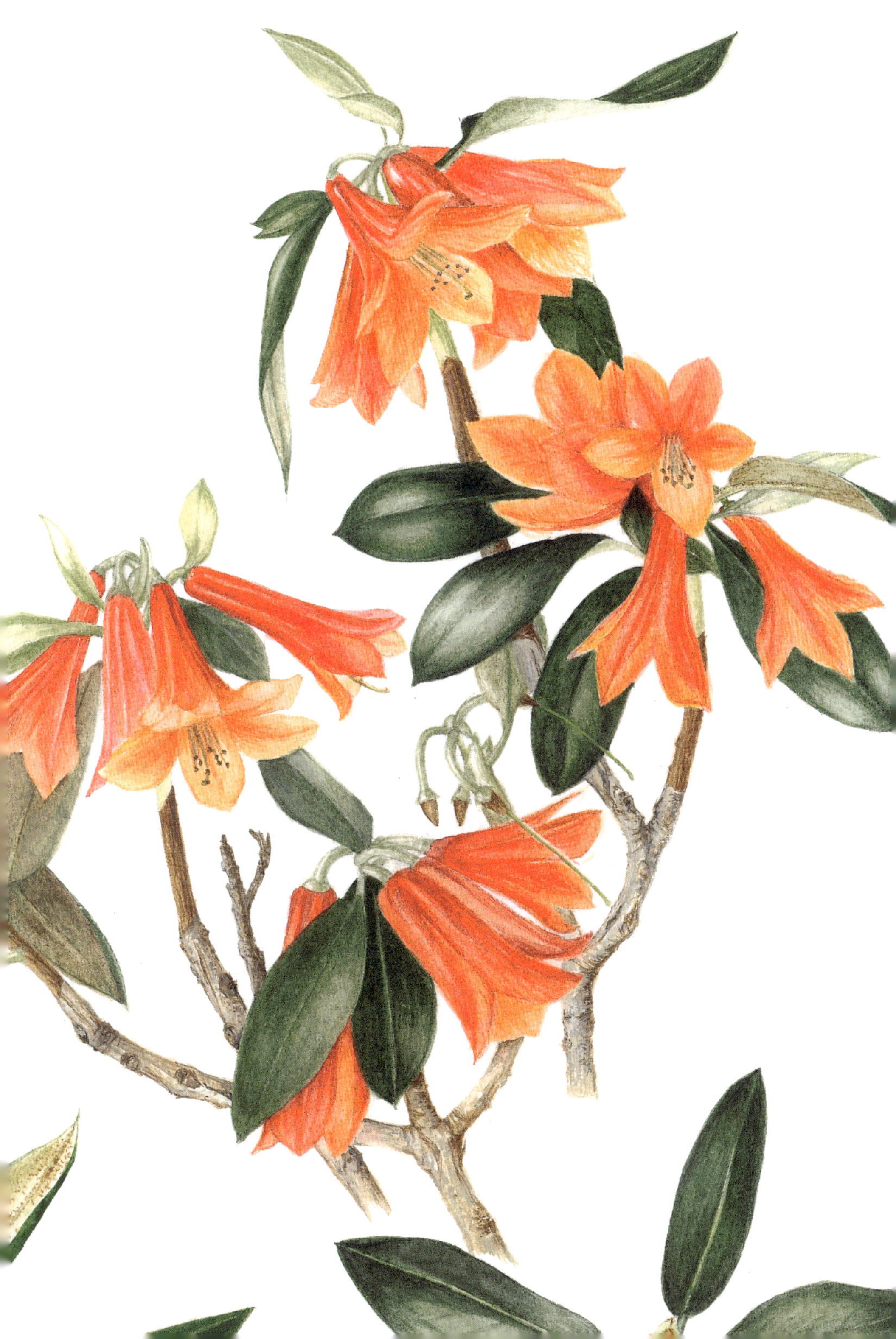

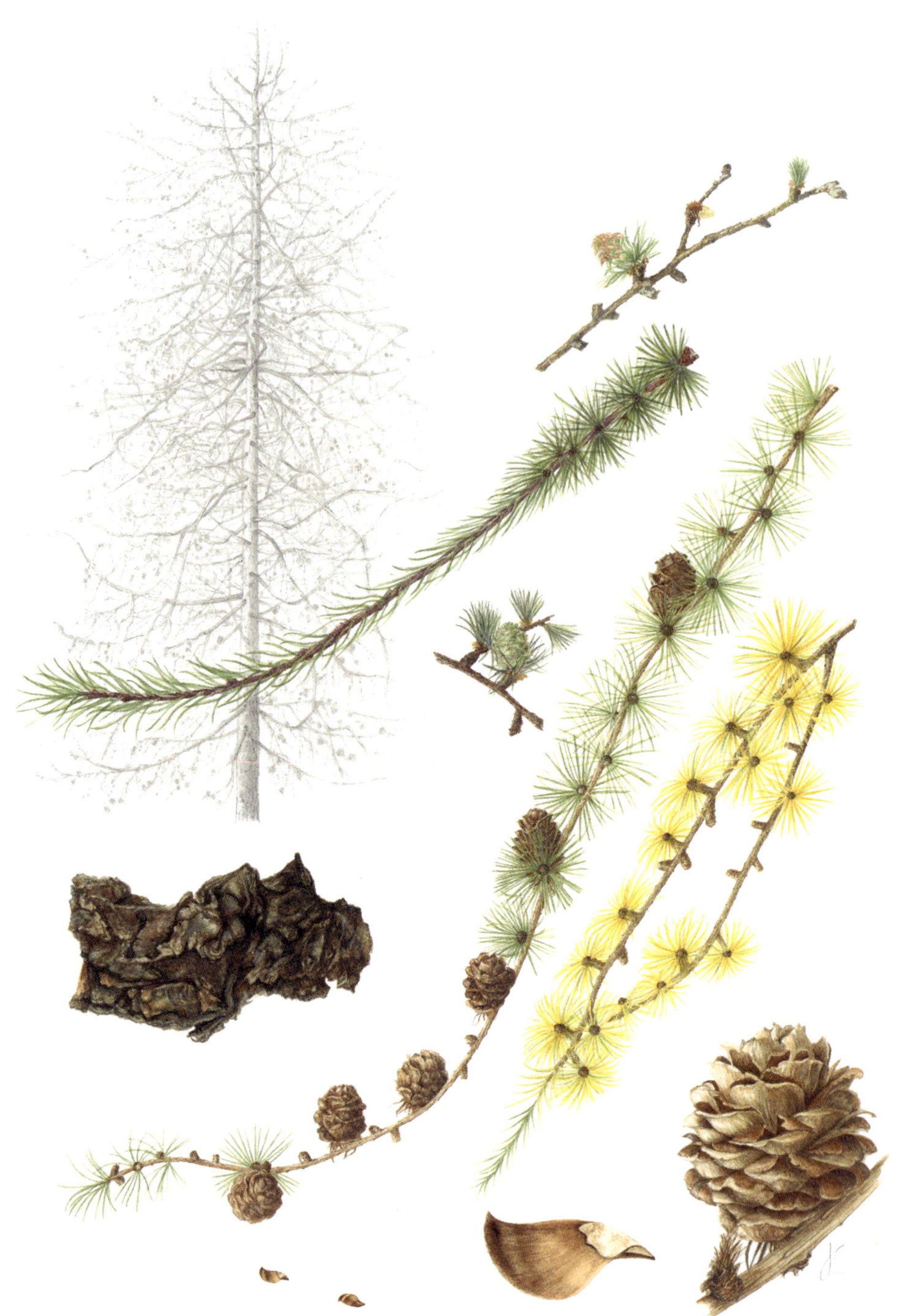

Larix kaempferi

Japanese larch

Not all conifers are evergreen. There are five types of deciduous conifer, of which this is an example. Bedgebury National Pinetum has all five.

Jackie Copeman, 2024
Watercolour and graphite pencil
on watercolour paper

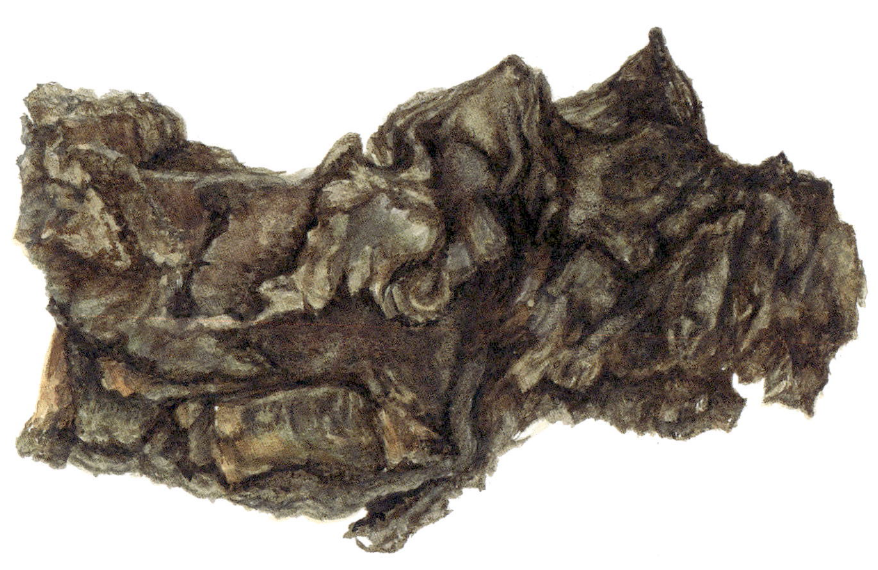

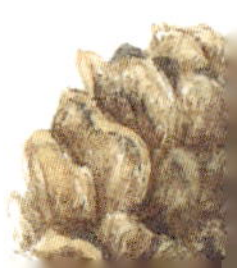

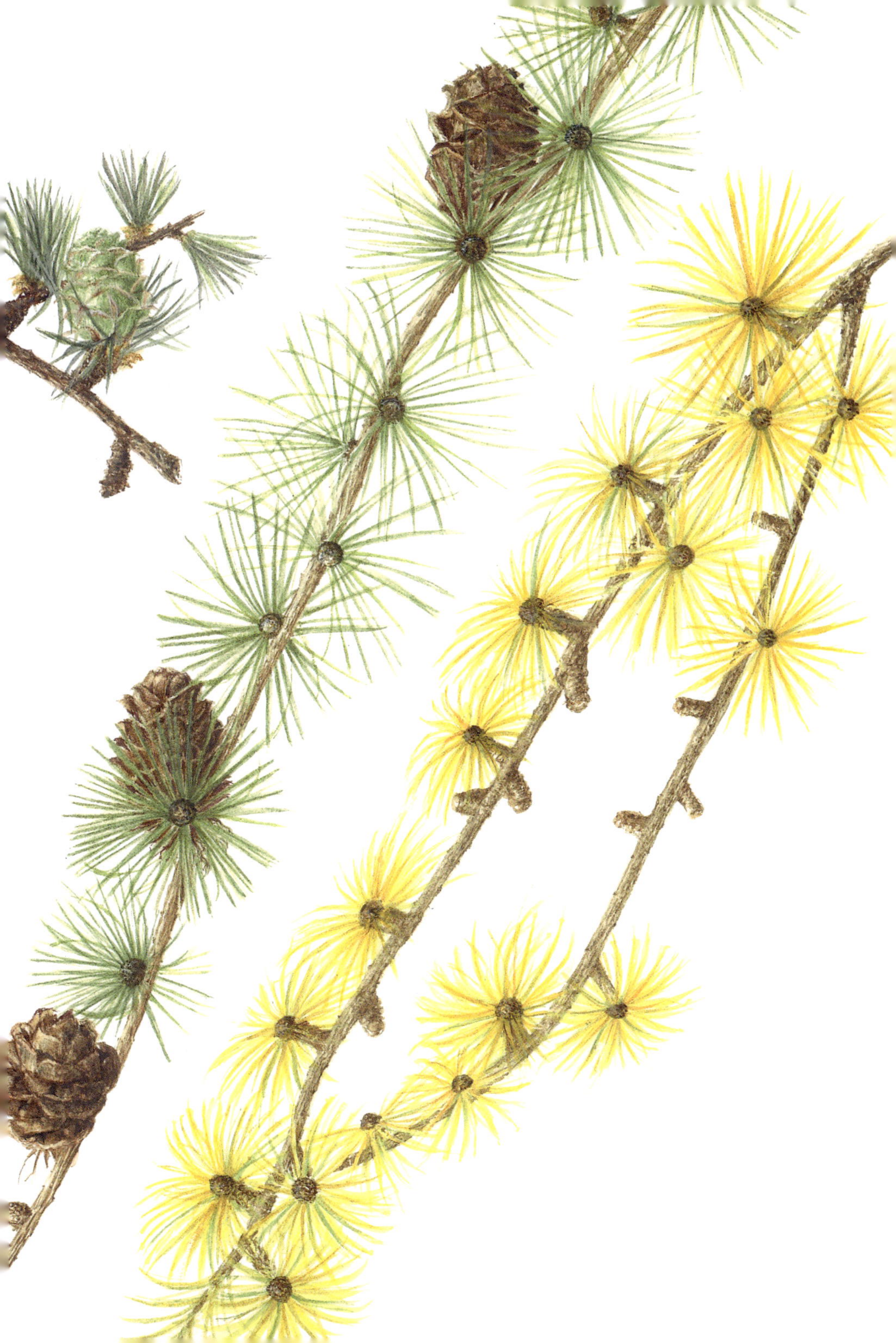

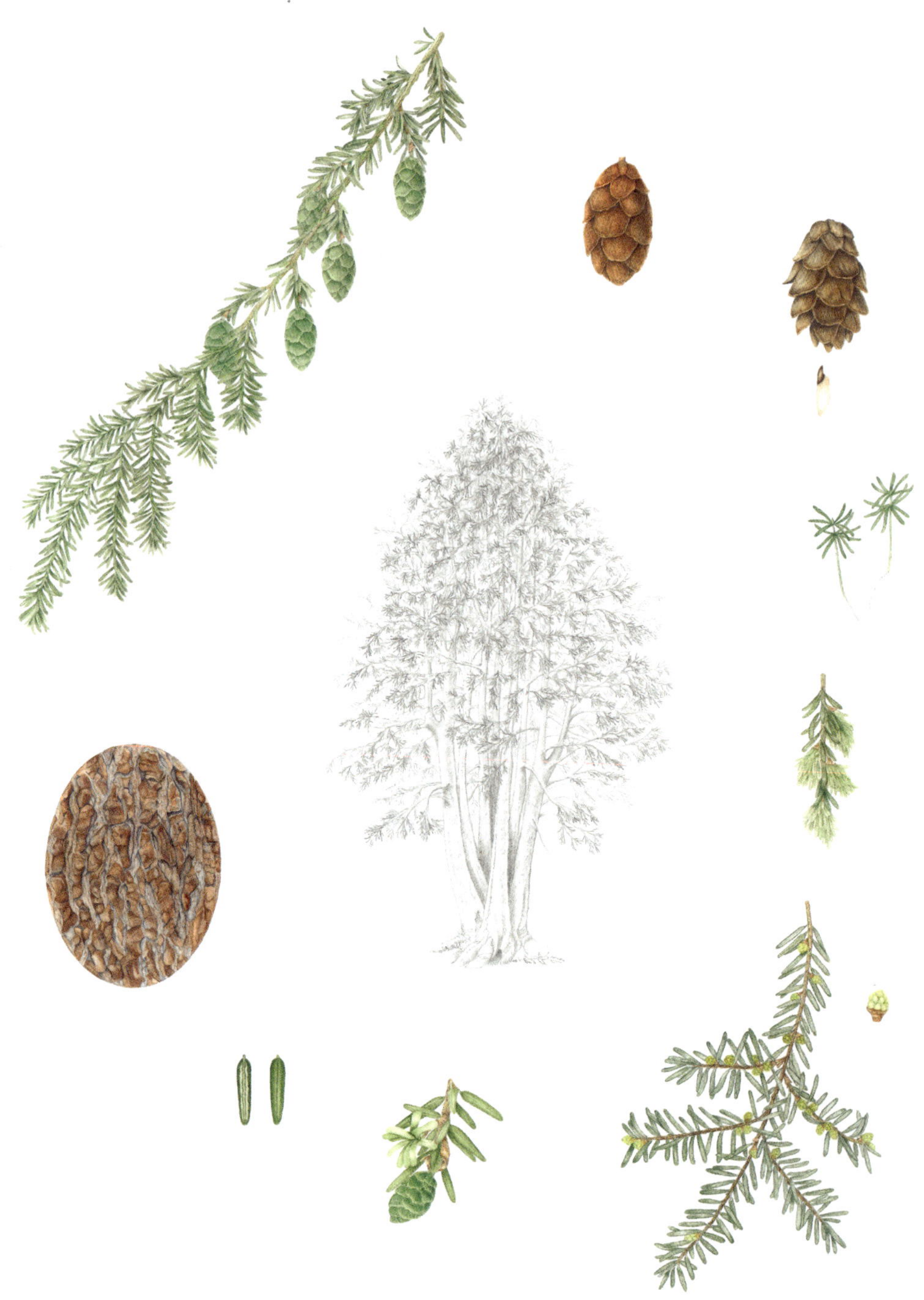

Tsuga canadensis
Eastern hemlock

Once common, this tree has been decimated in recent times by a combination of introduced pests and climate change. Originating in east coast USA, a number of these were collected in 2006 by Bedgebury National Pinetum staff.

Louisa Bailey, 2024
Watercolour and graphite pencil on watercolour paper

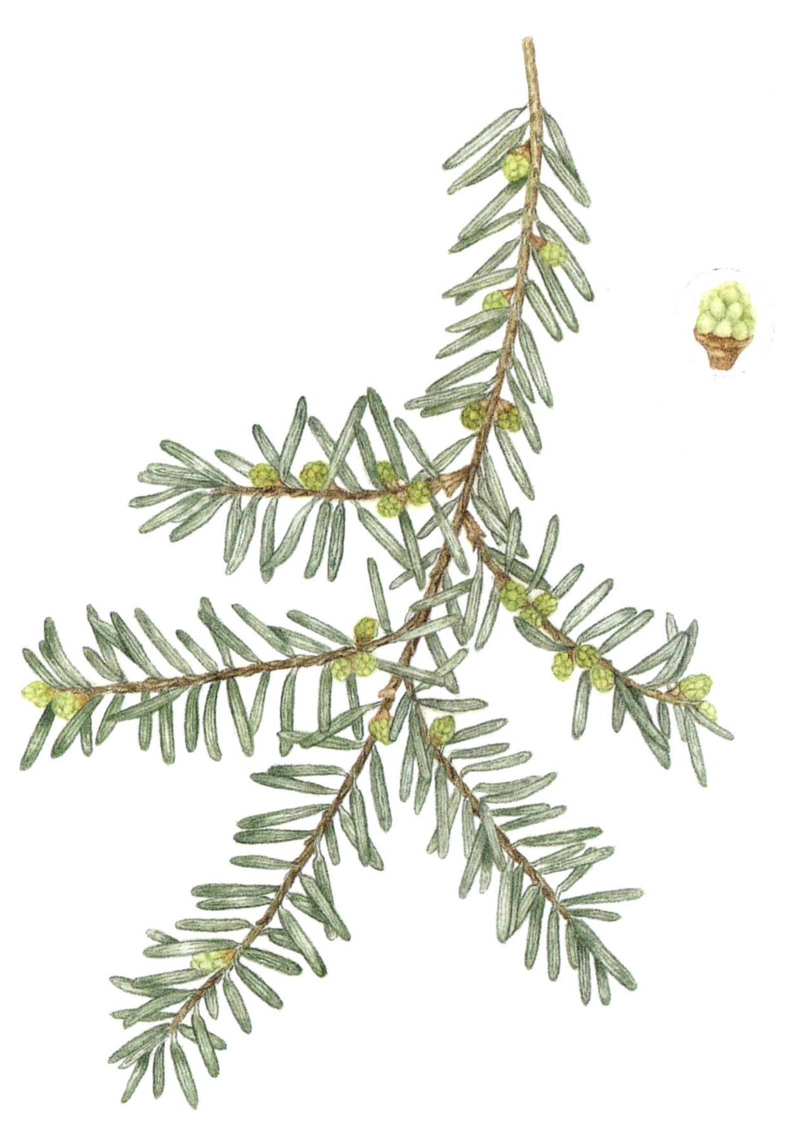

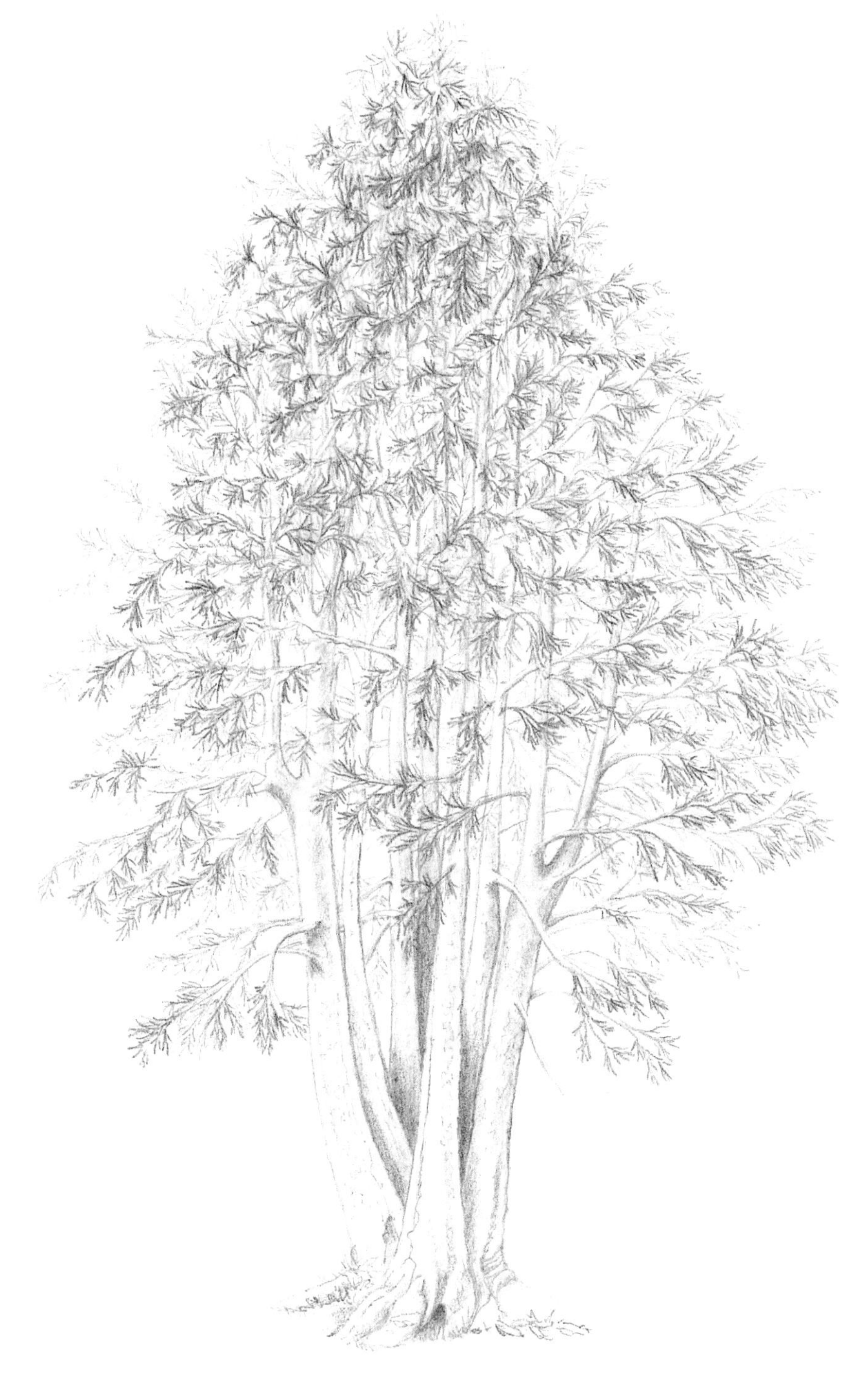

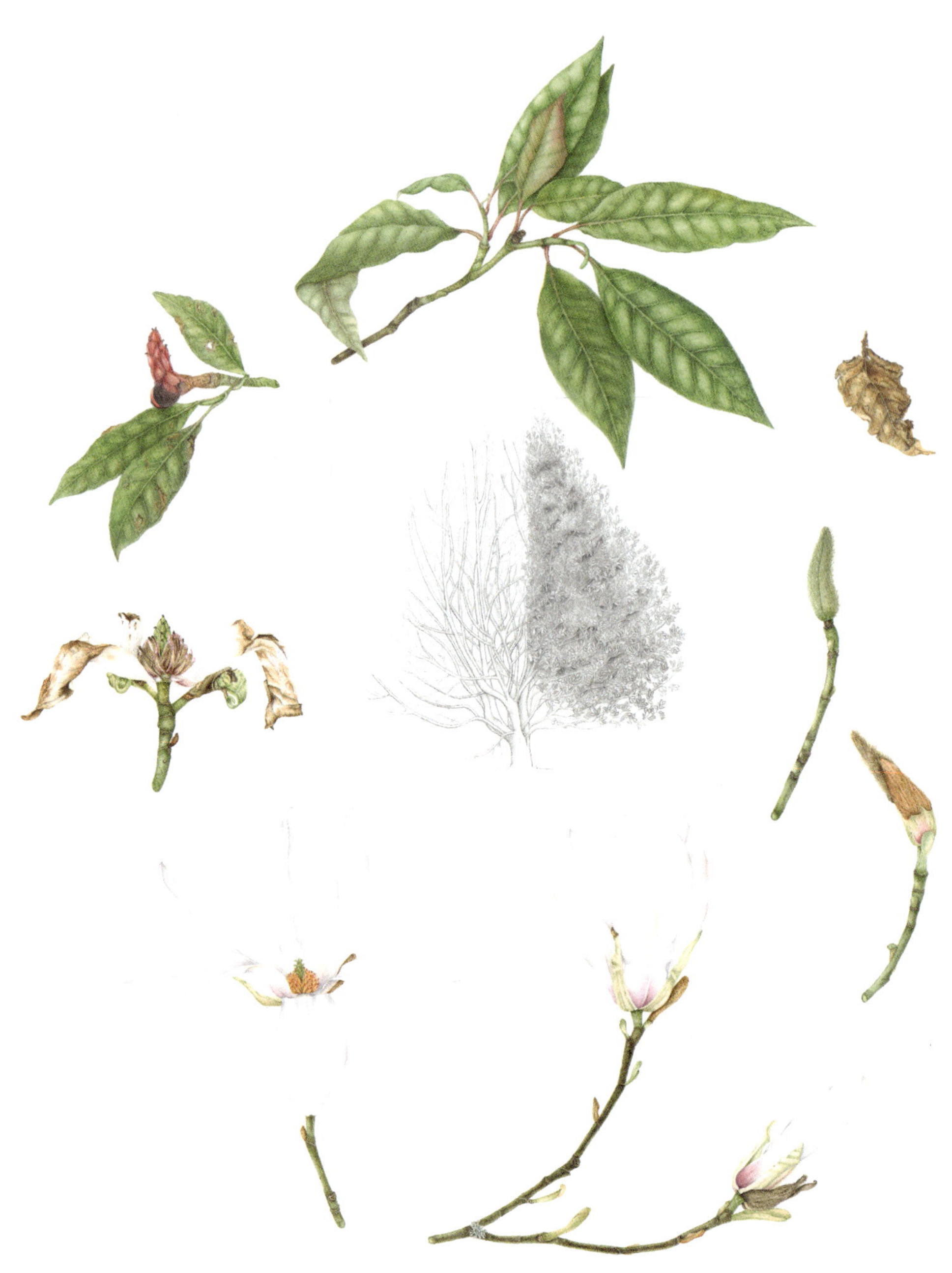

Magnolia salicifolia
Willow-leaved magnolia

Grown as an ornamental shrub, this species produces beautiful flowers in spring. Bedgebury National Pinetum grows it to provide seasonal interest for visitors.

Louisa Bailey, 2024
Watercolour and graphite pencil on watercolour paper

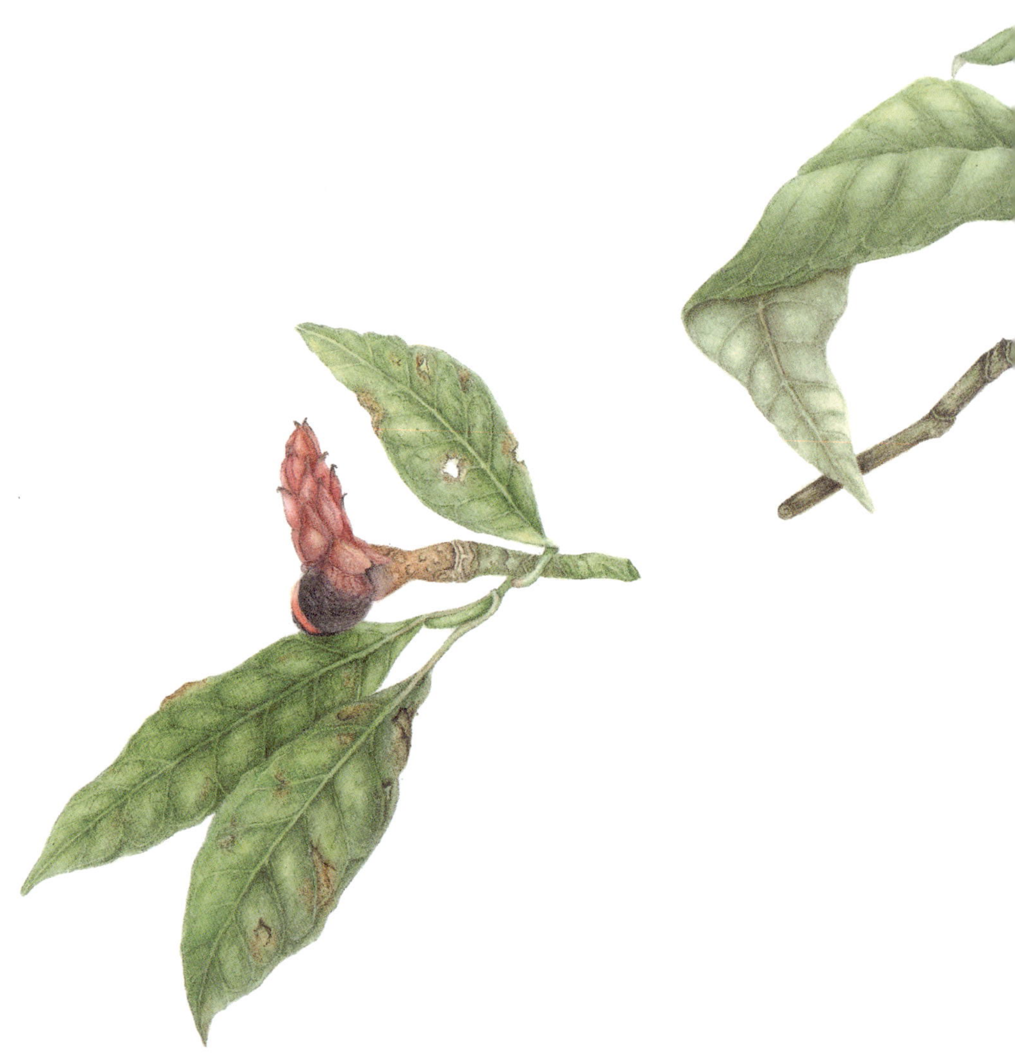

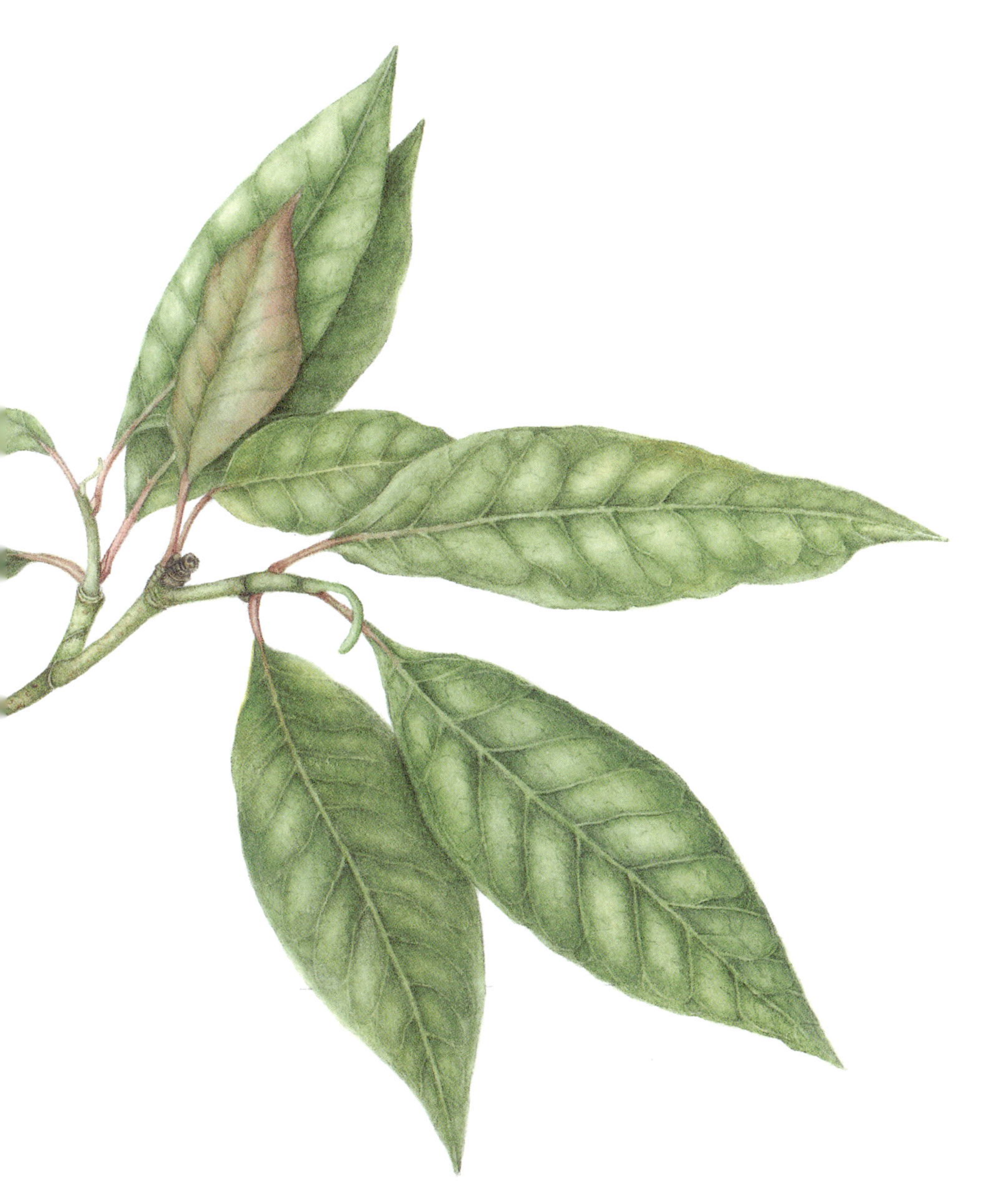

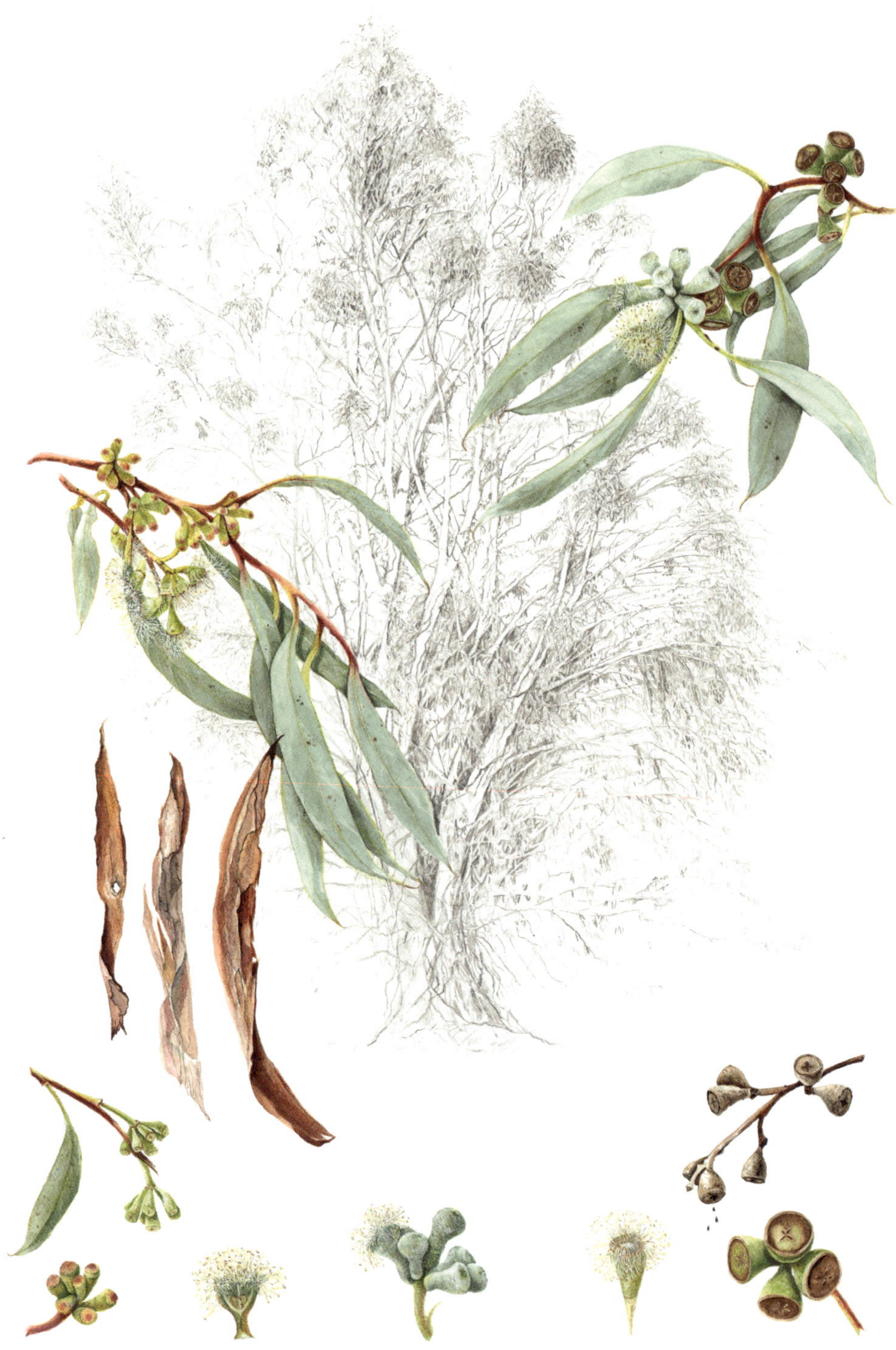

Eucalyptus coccifera
Tasmanian snow gum
Bedgebury National Pinetum is assessing a number of eucalyptus species, including this one, for potential use in forestry and as a source of biomass fuel.

Helen Hiorns, 2024
Watercolour and graphite pencil on watercolour paper

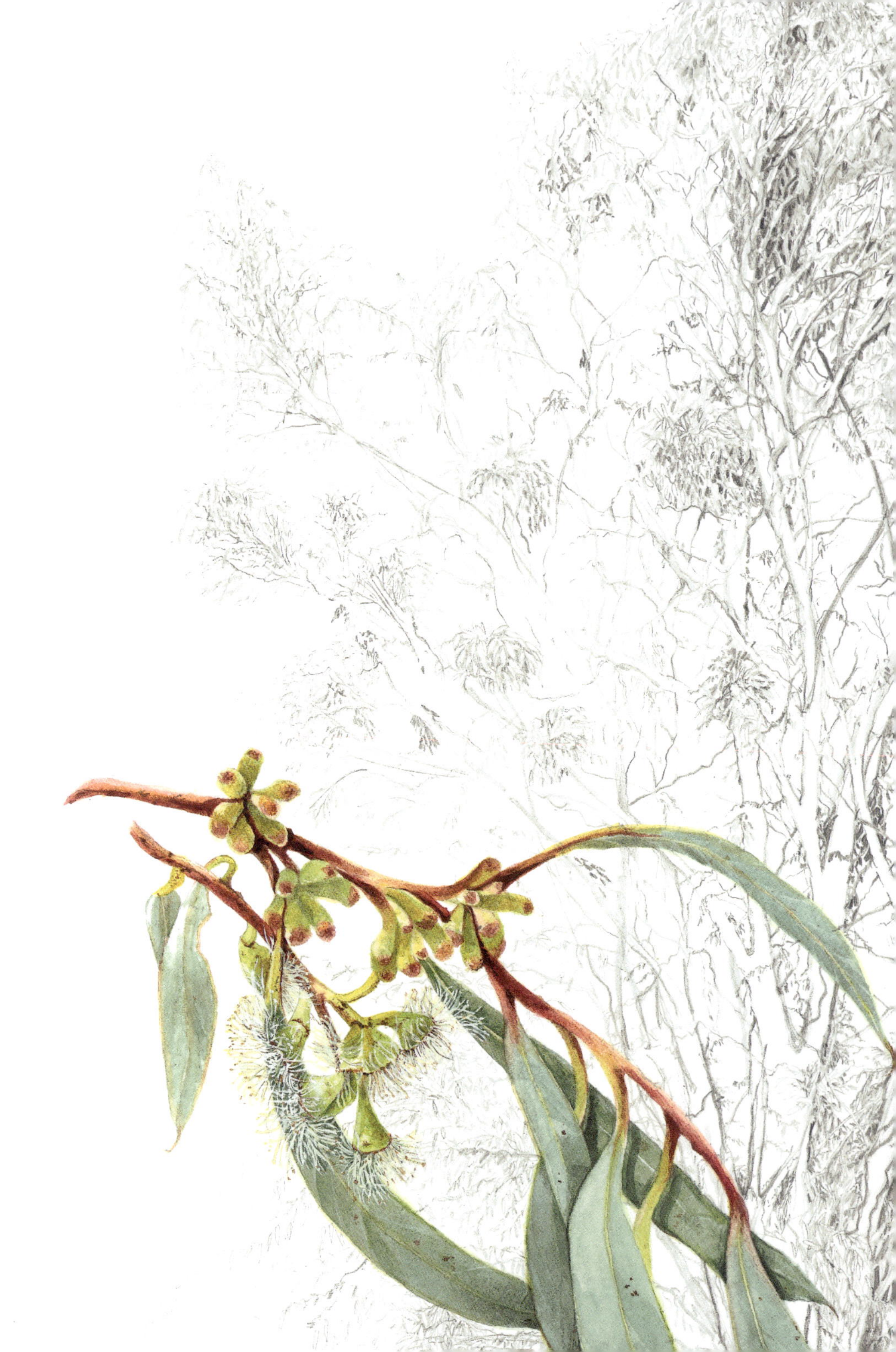

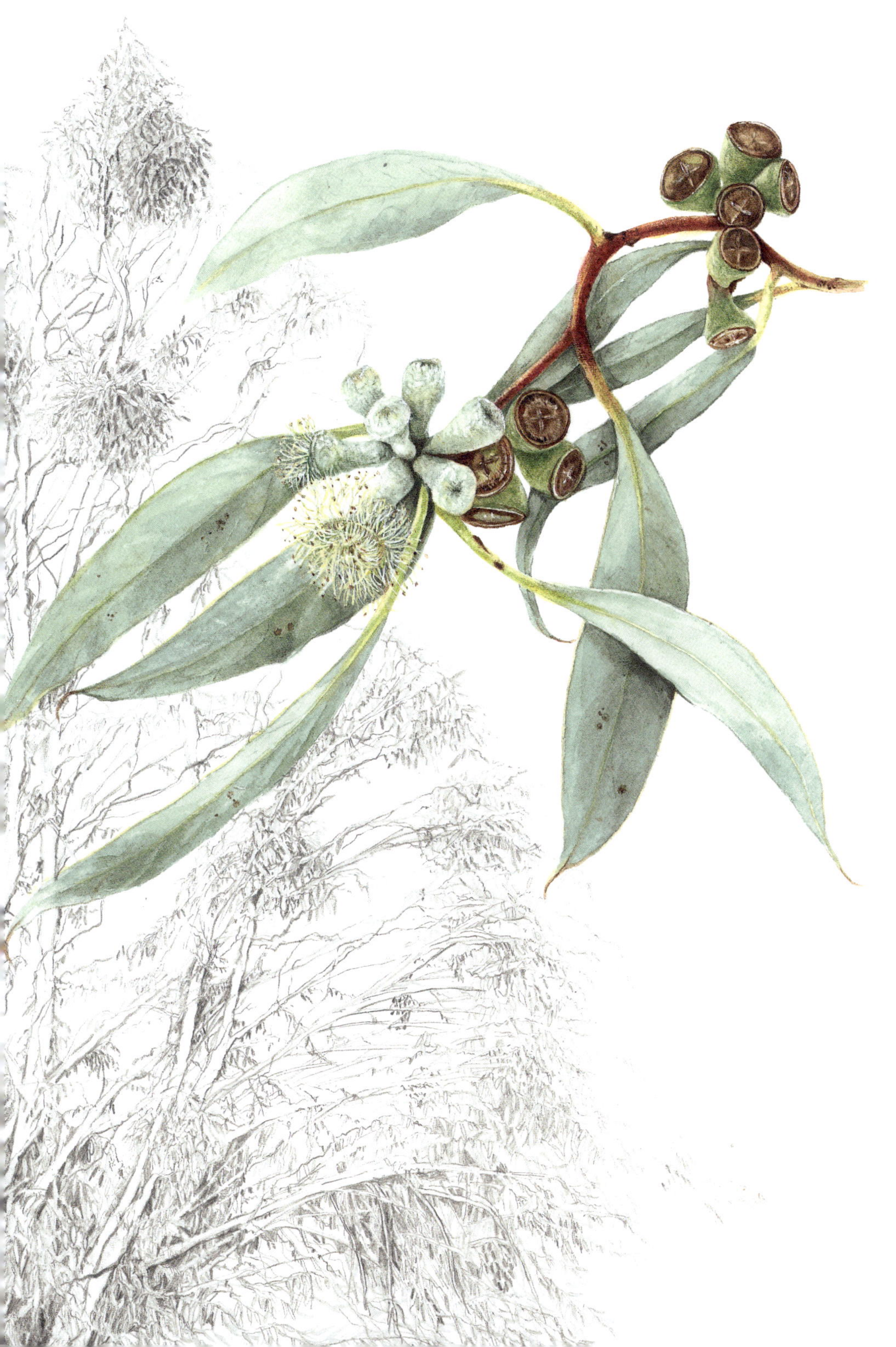

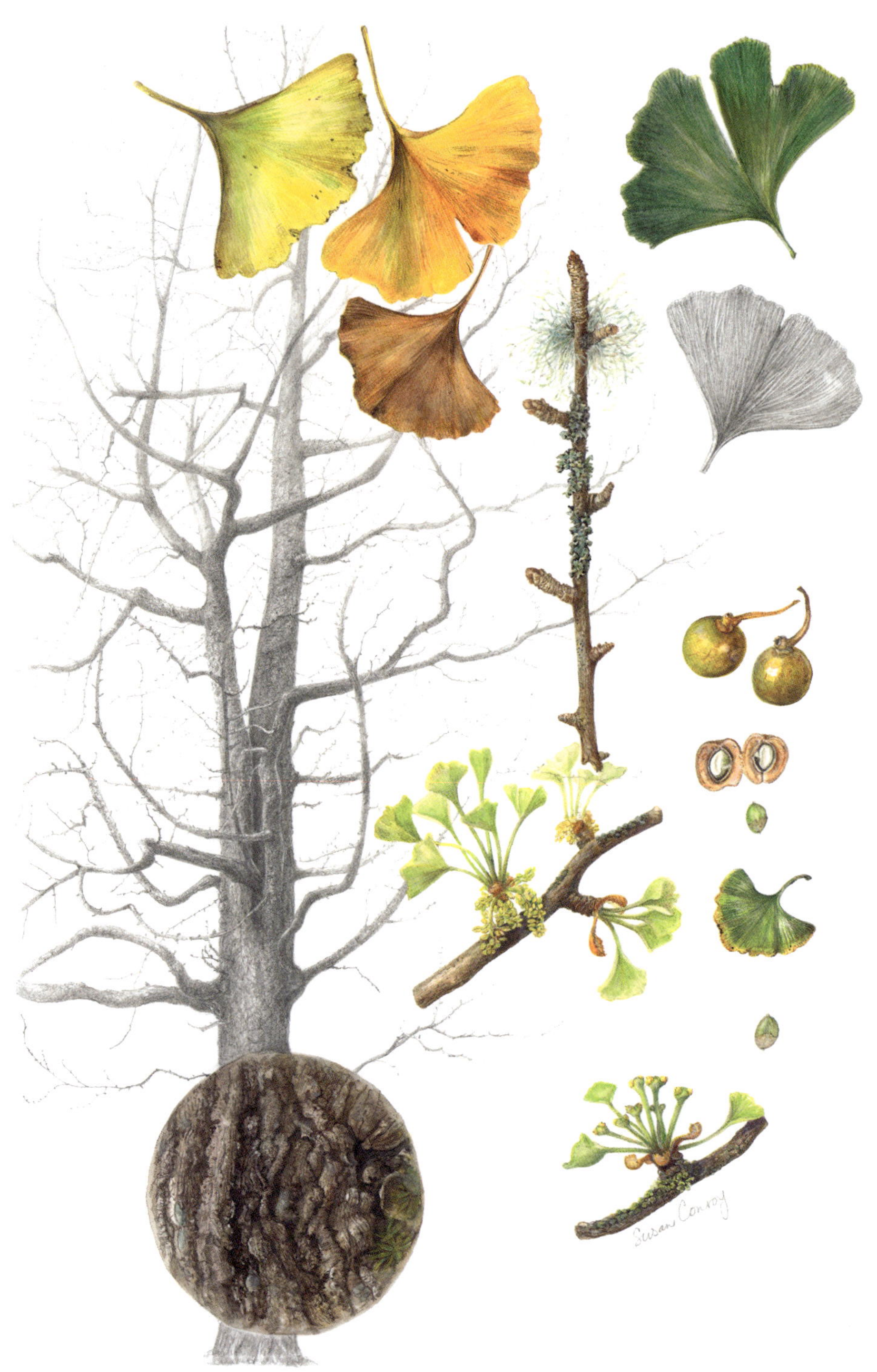
Susan Conroy

Ginkgo biloba

Maidenhair tree

This close relative of conifers is one of the most ancient types of tree. Ginkgos are very tolerant of pollution; some even survived the Hiroshima atomic bomb. This quality makes them very useful as street trees around the world.

Susan Conroy, 2024
Watercolour and graphite pencil
on watercolour paper

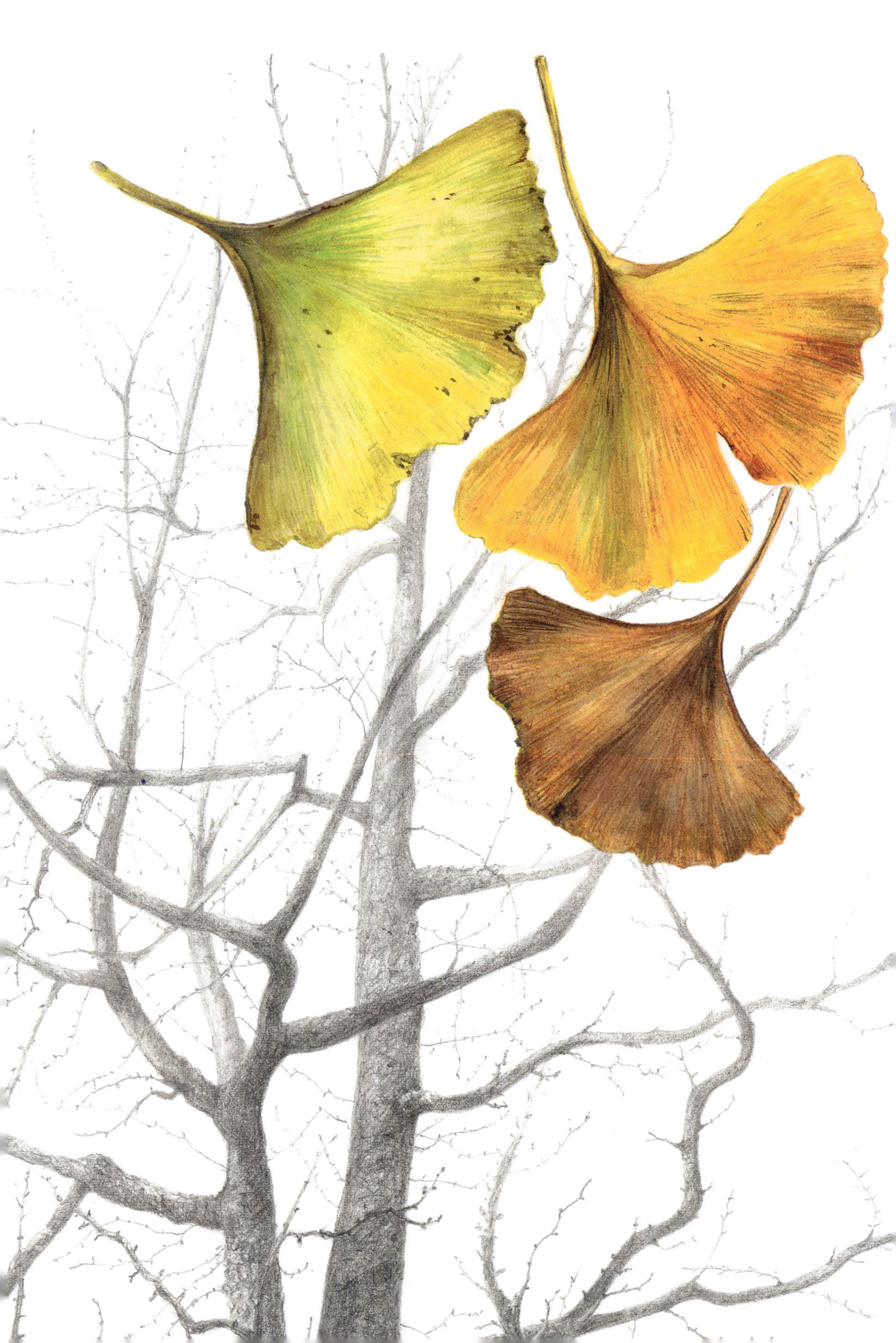

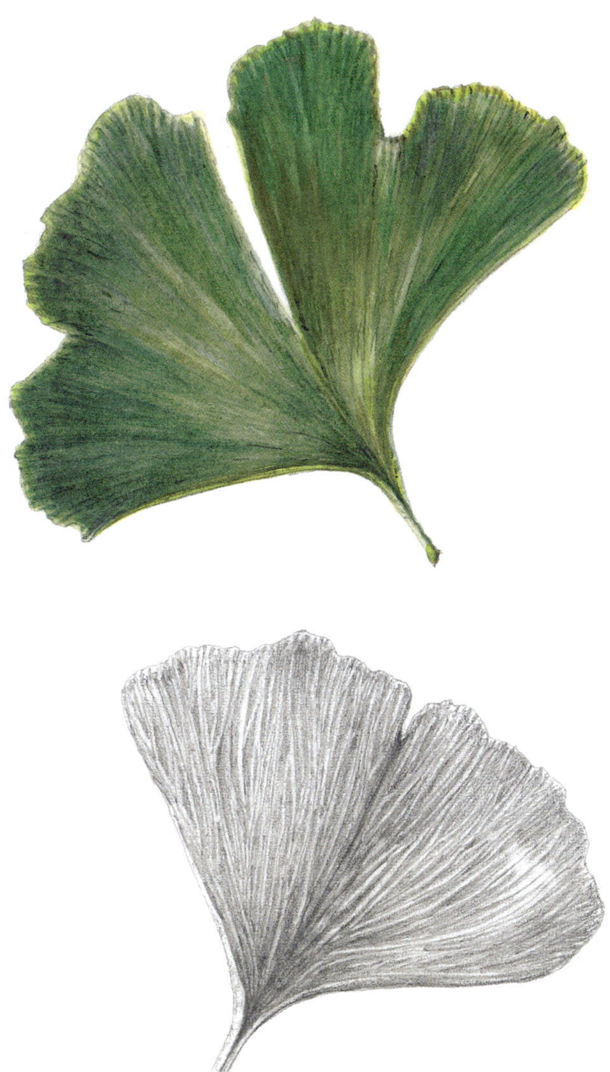

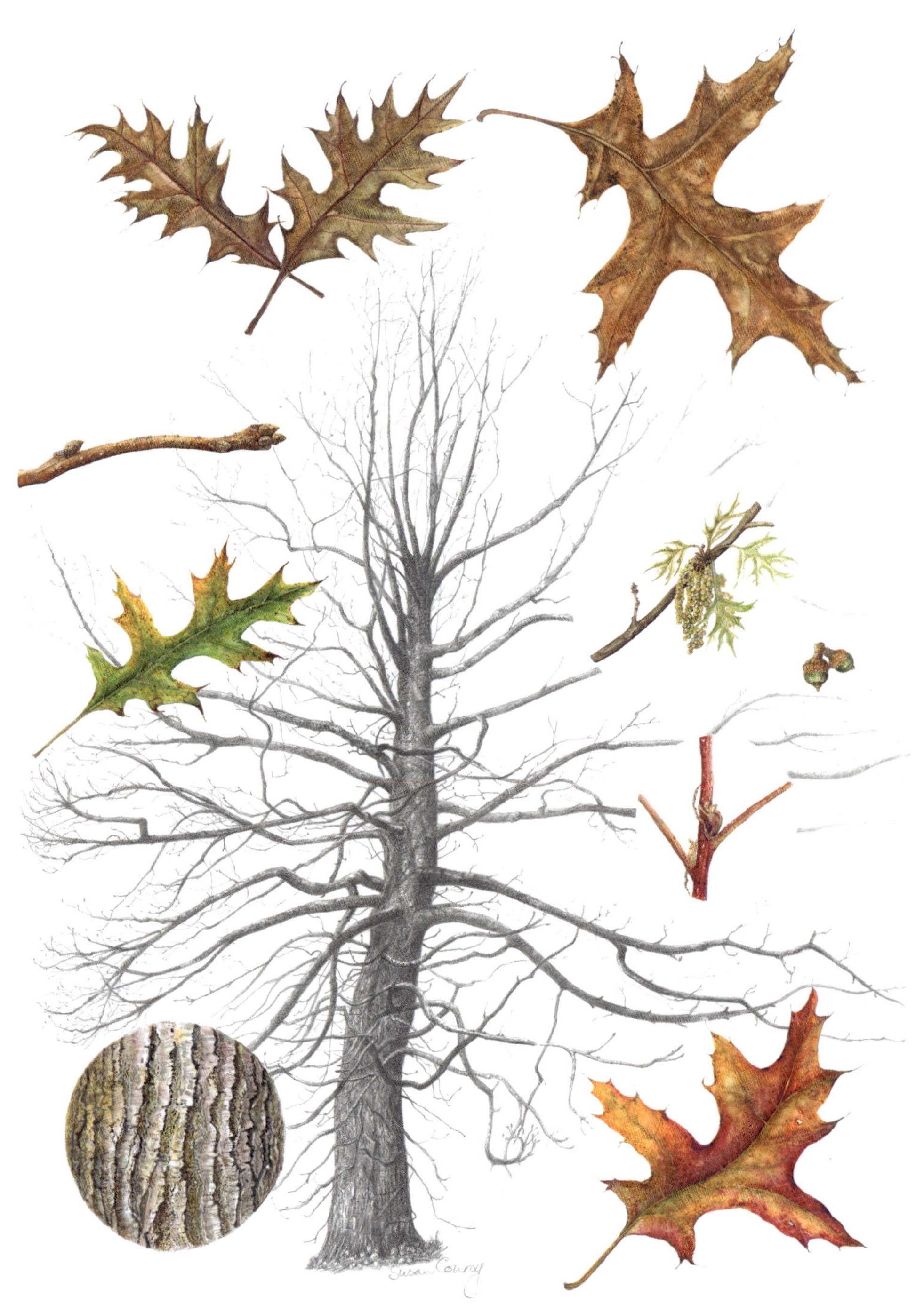

Quercus palustris

Pin oak

A potential timber tree of the future which is fairly quick growing and tolerant of pollution. It grows well in warmer climates and is also tolerant of acidic soils. Some have great autumn colour.

Susan Conroy, 2024
Watercolour and graphite pencil on watercolour paper

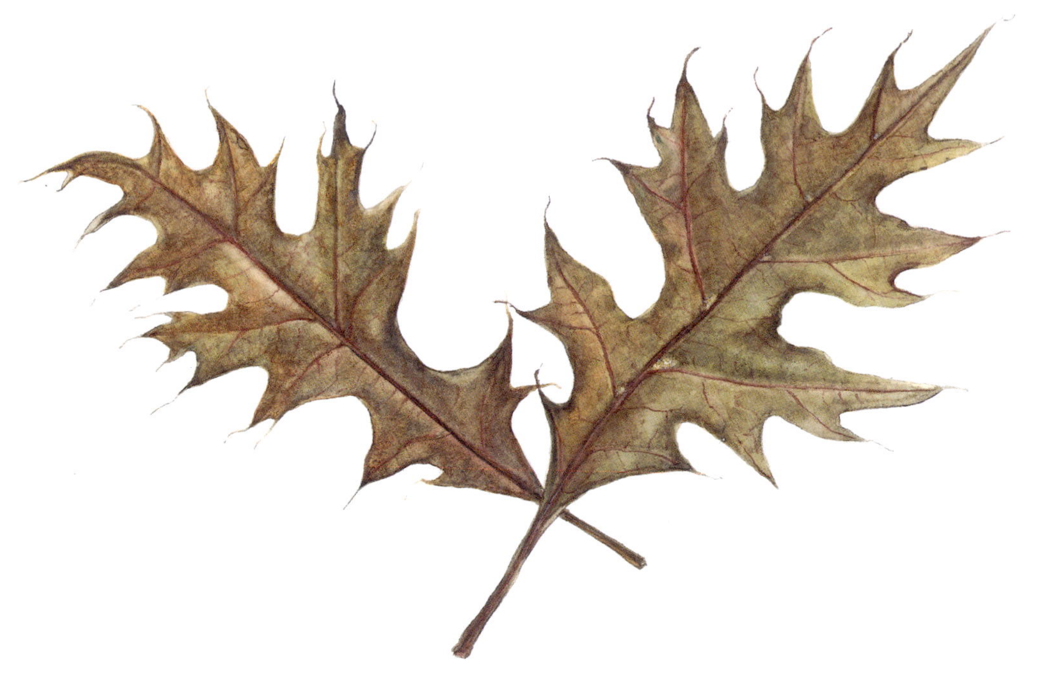

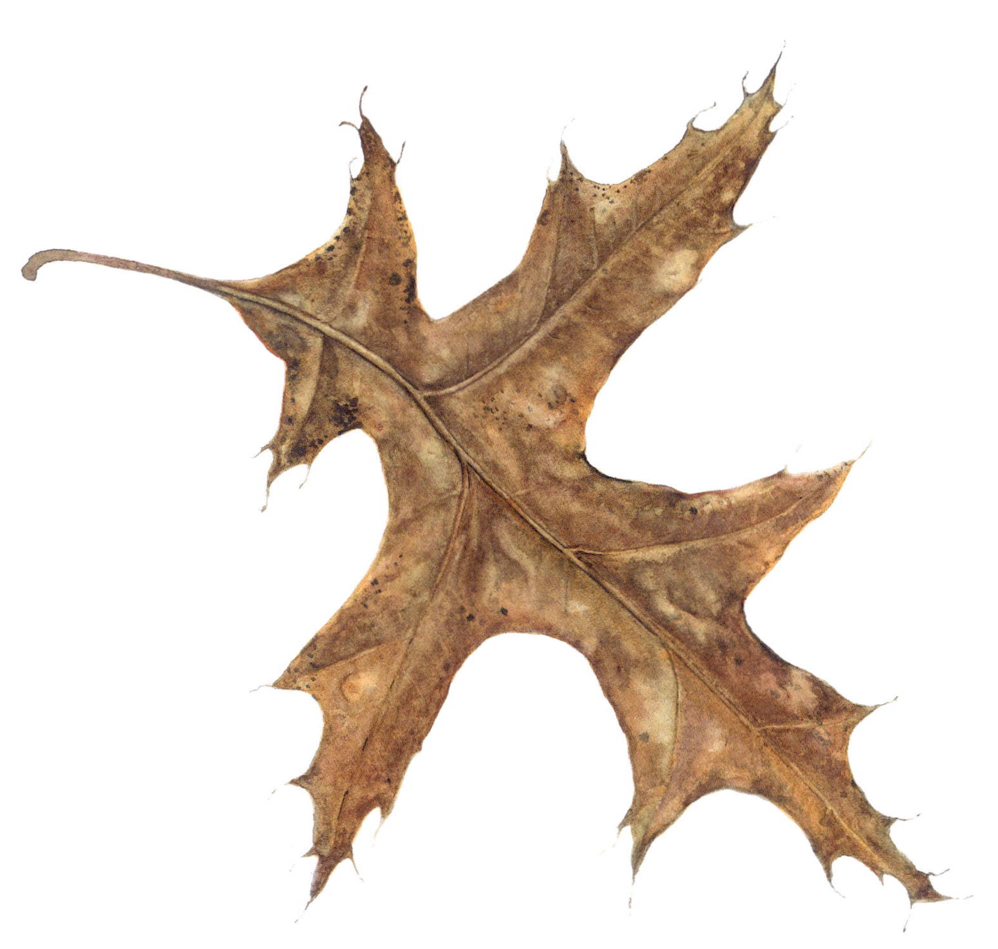

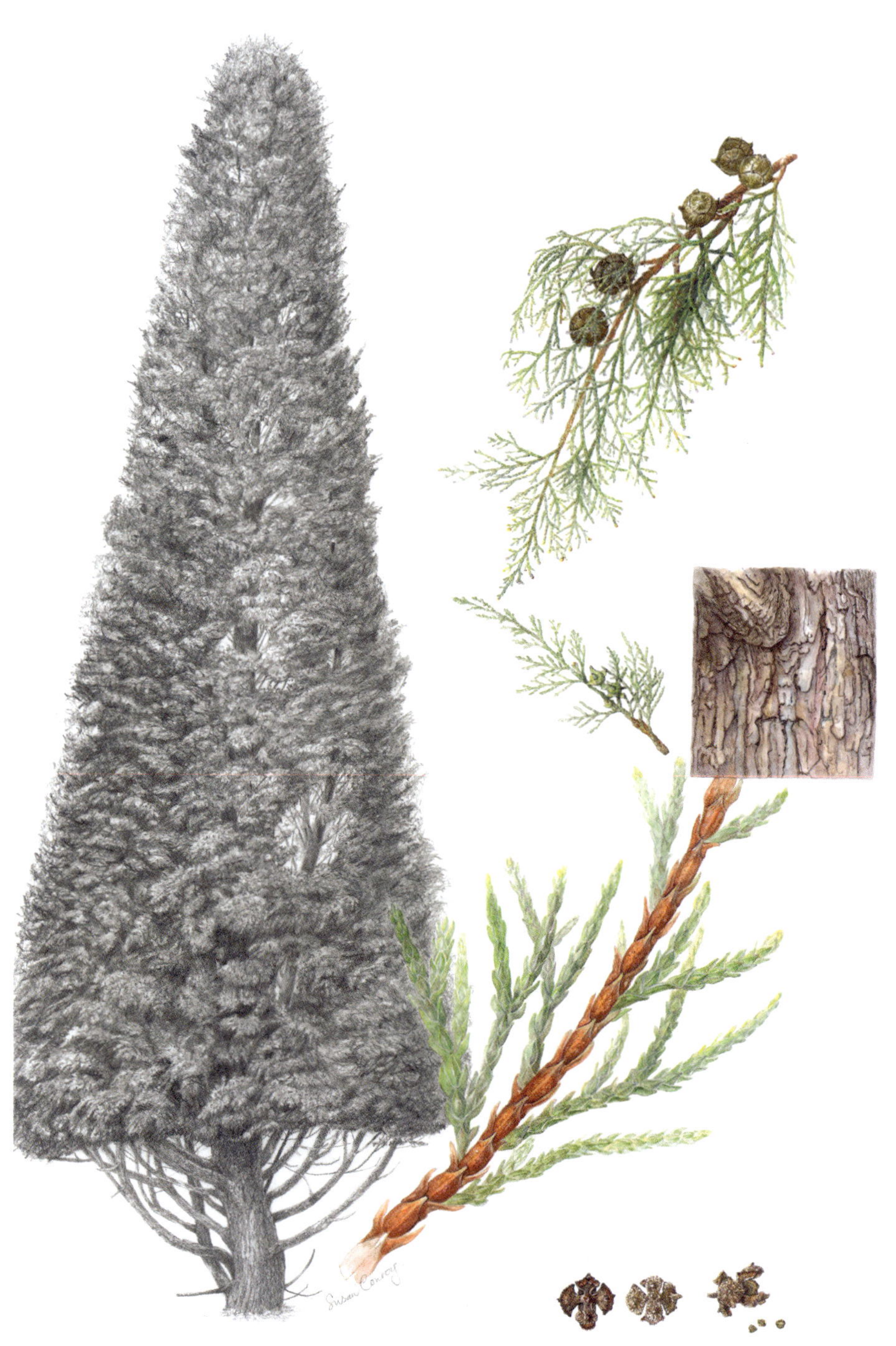
Susan Conroy

x *Hesperotropsis leylandii*
(x *Cupressocyparis leylandii*)
Leyland cypress

This tree's rapid growth and height has gained it a bad reputation, but that's down to its misuse in urban landscapes. Today, Bedgebury holds the Plant Heritage National Collection of Leyland cypresses, a comprehensive living library containing many of the known cultivars.

Susan Conroy, 2024
Watercolour and graphite pencil on watercolour paper

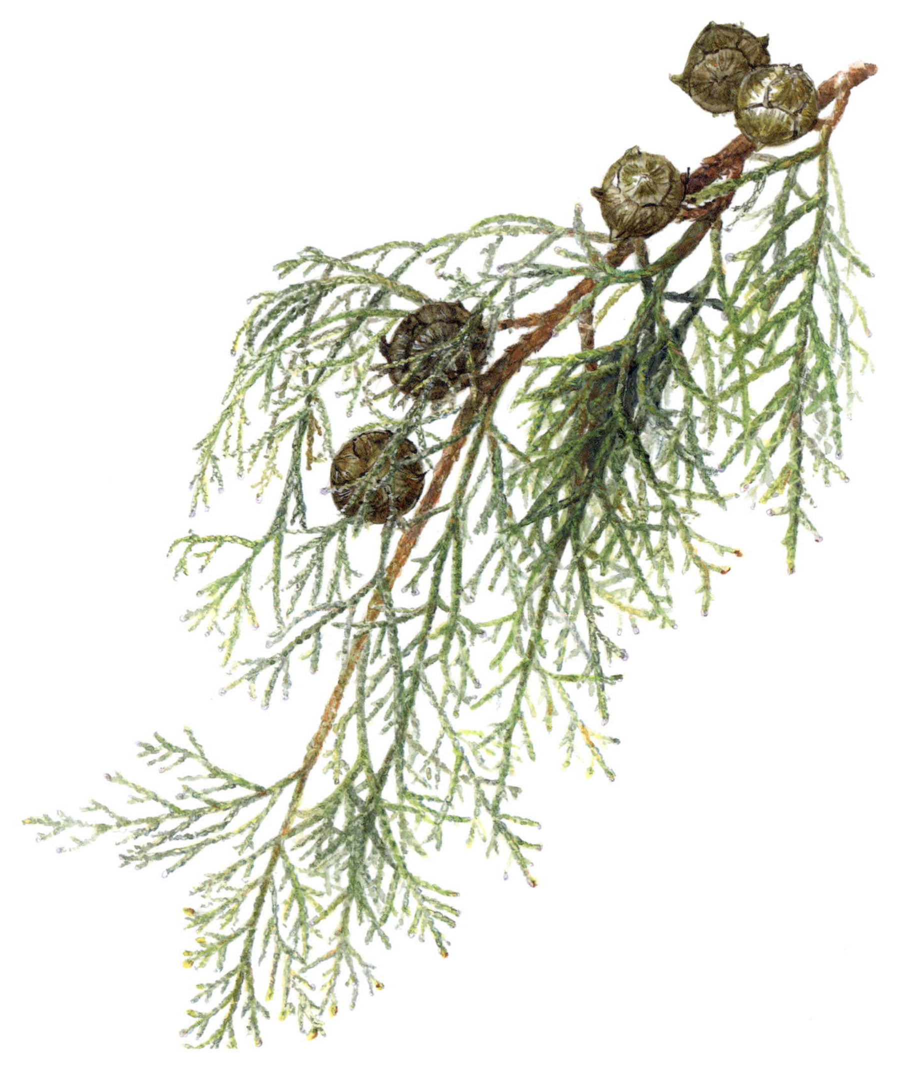

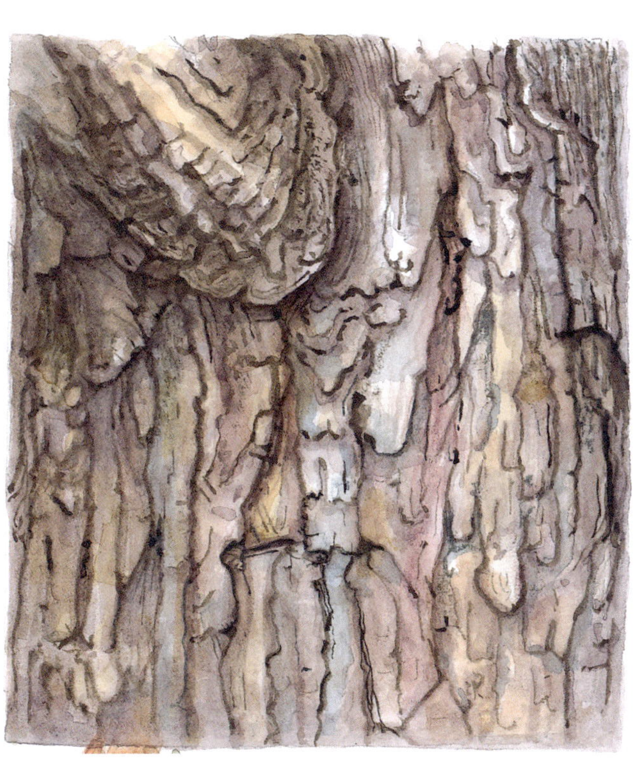

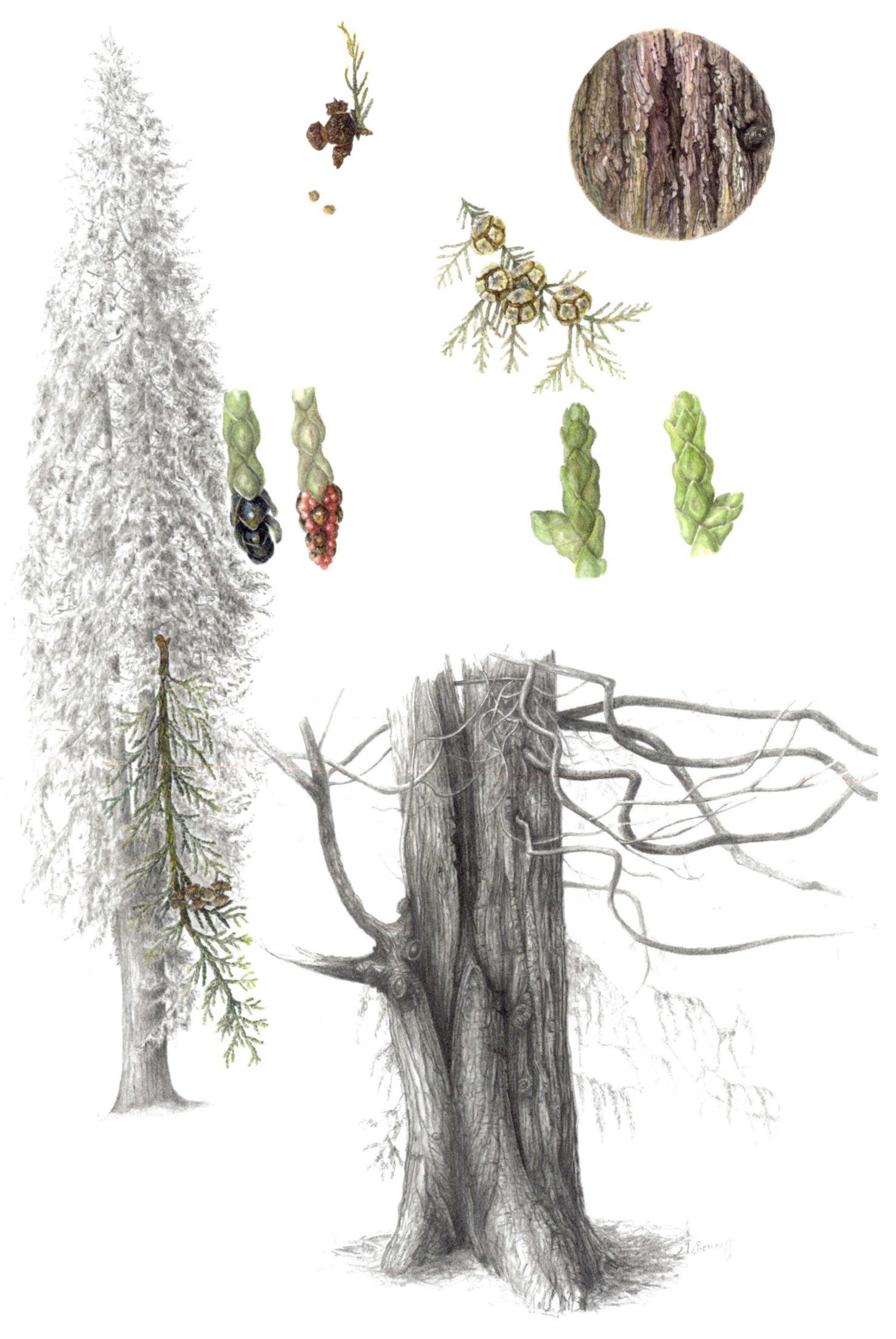

Chamaecyparis lawsoniana
Lawson's cypress

An avenue of Lawson cypresses forms a link between Bedgebury National Pinetum's past and present. Planted in 1870, it pre-dates the formation of the pinetum and was named Lady Mildred's Carriage Drive after the wife of a previous owner.

Susan Conroy, 2024
Watercolour and graphite pencil
on watercolour paper

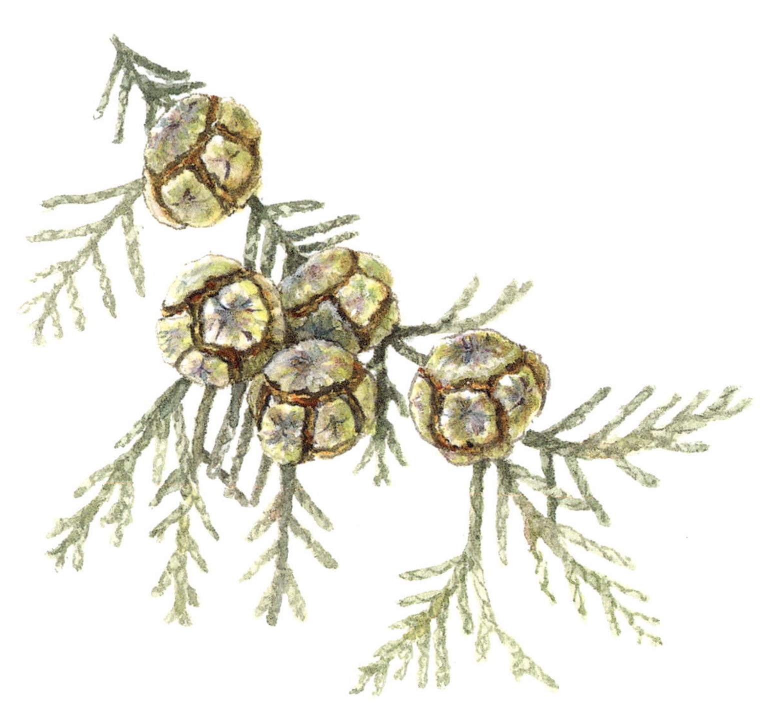

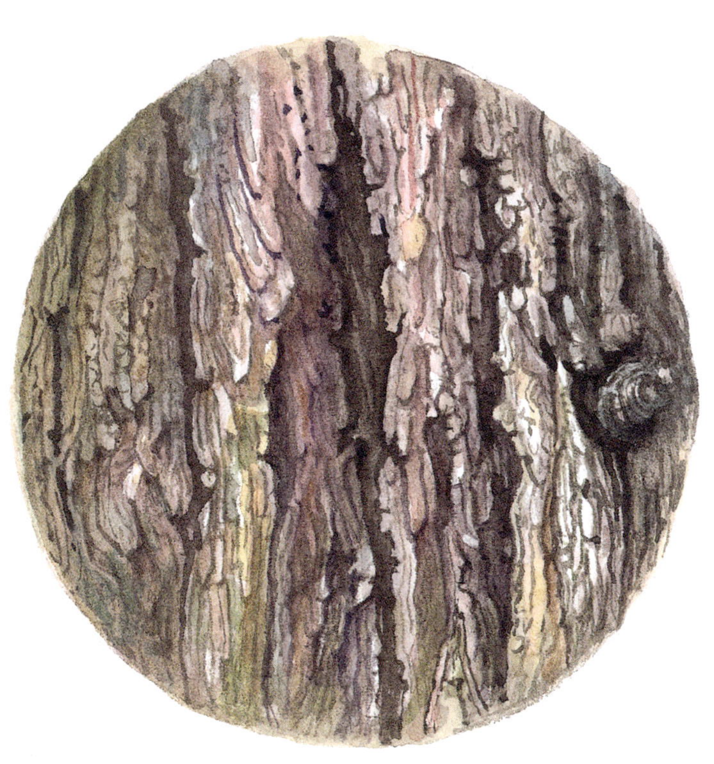

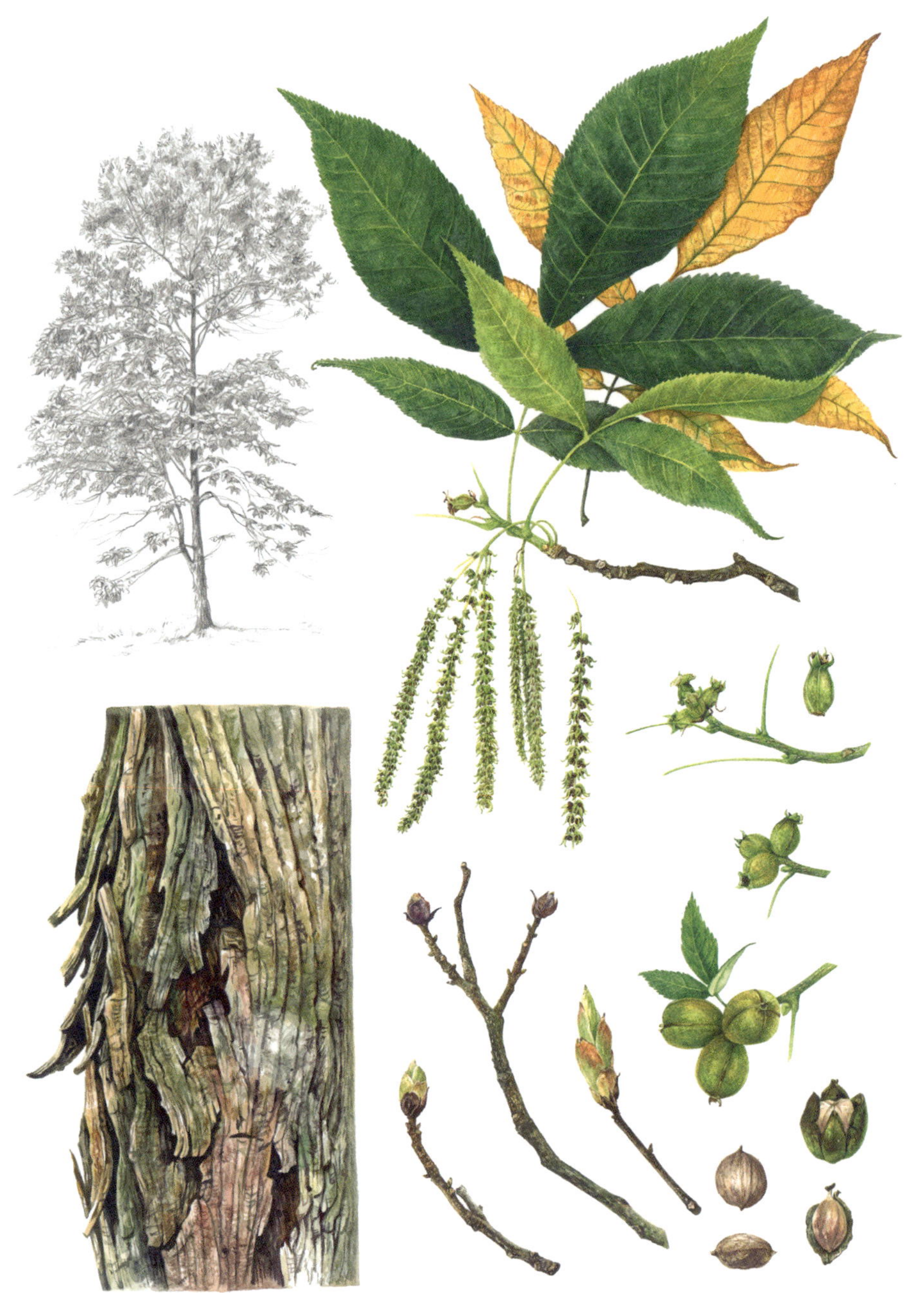

Carya ovata
Shagbark hickory
This tree provides beautiful autumn colour and has potential as a future timber and landscape species in a changing climate.

Sandra Fernandez, 2024
Watercolour and graphite pencil
on watercolour paper

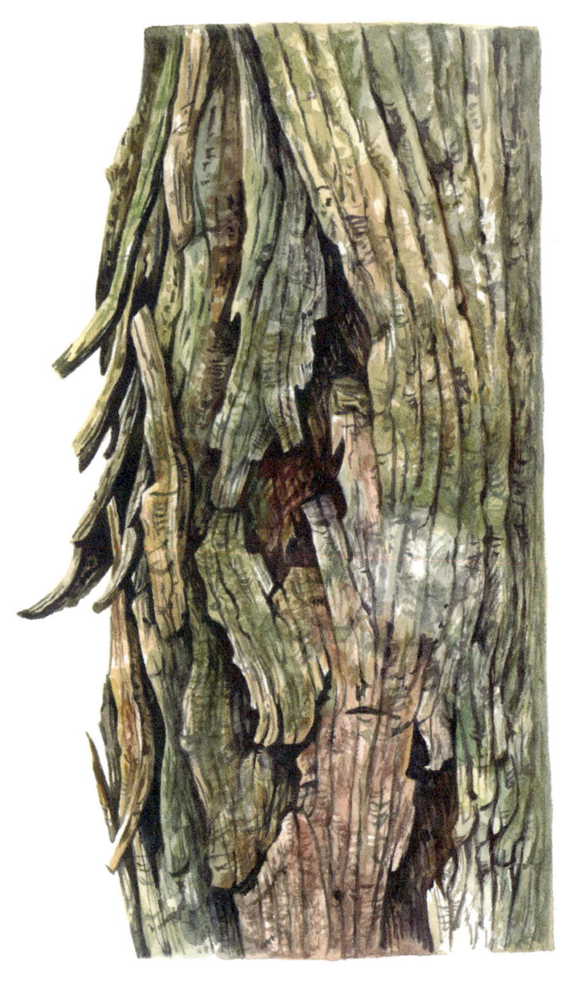

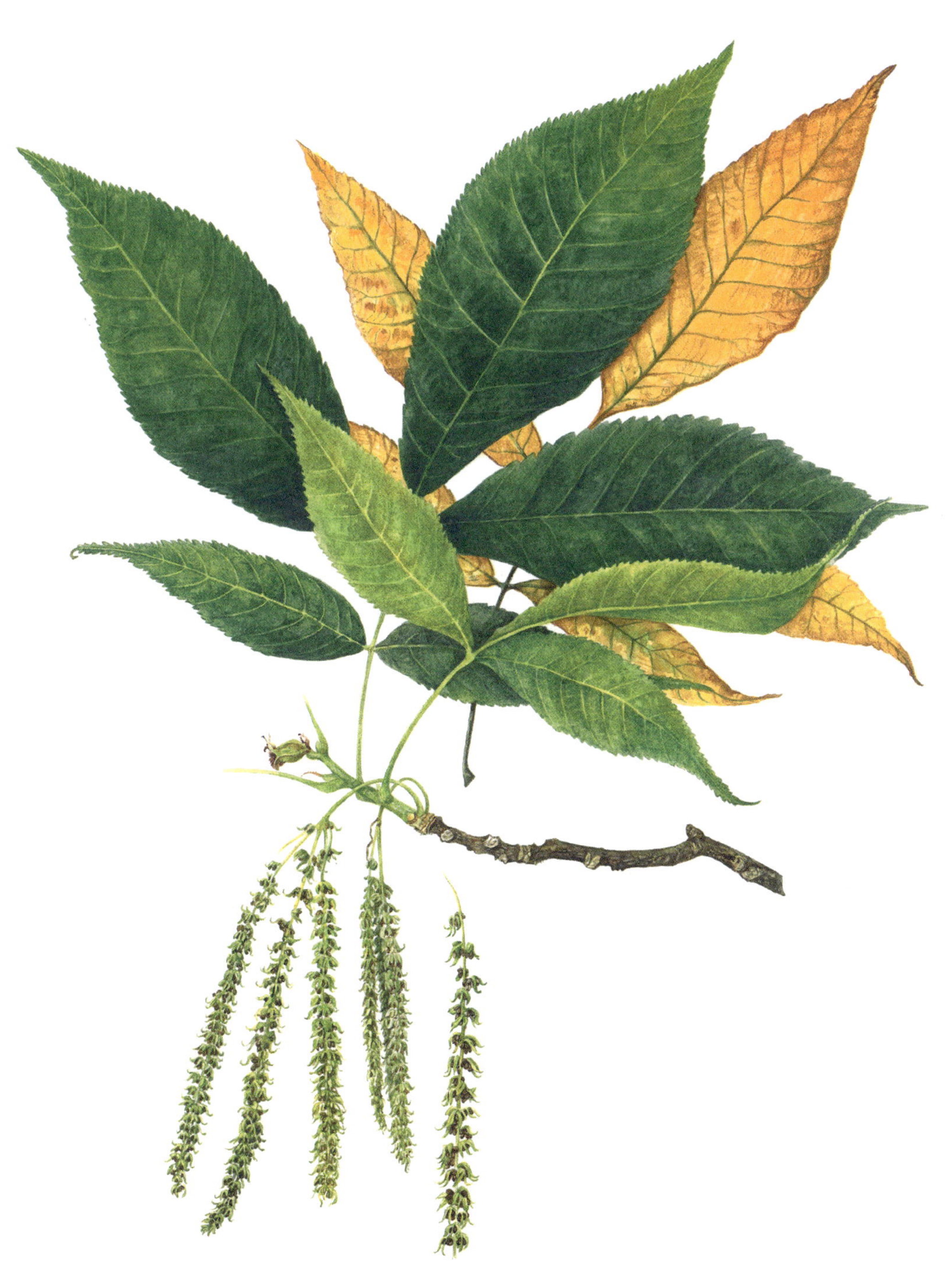

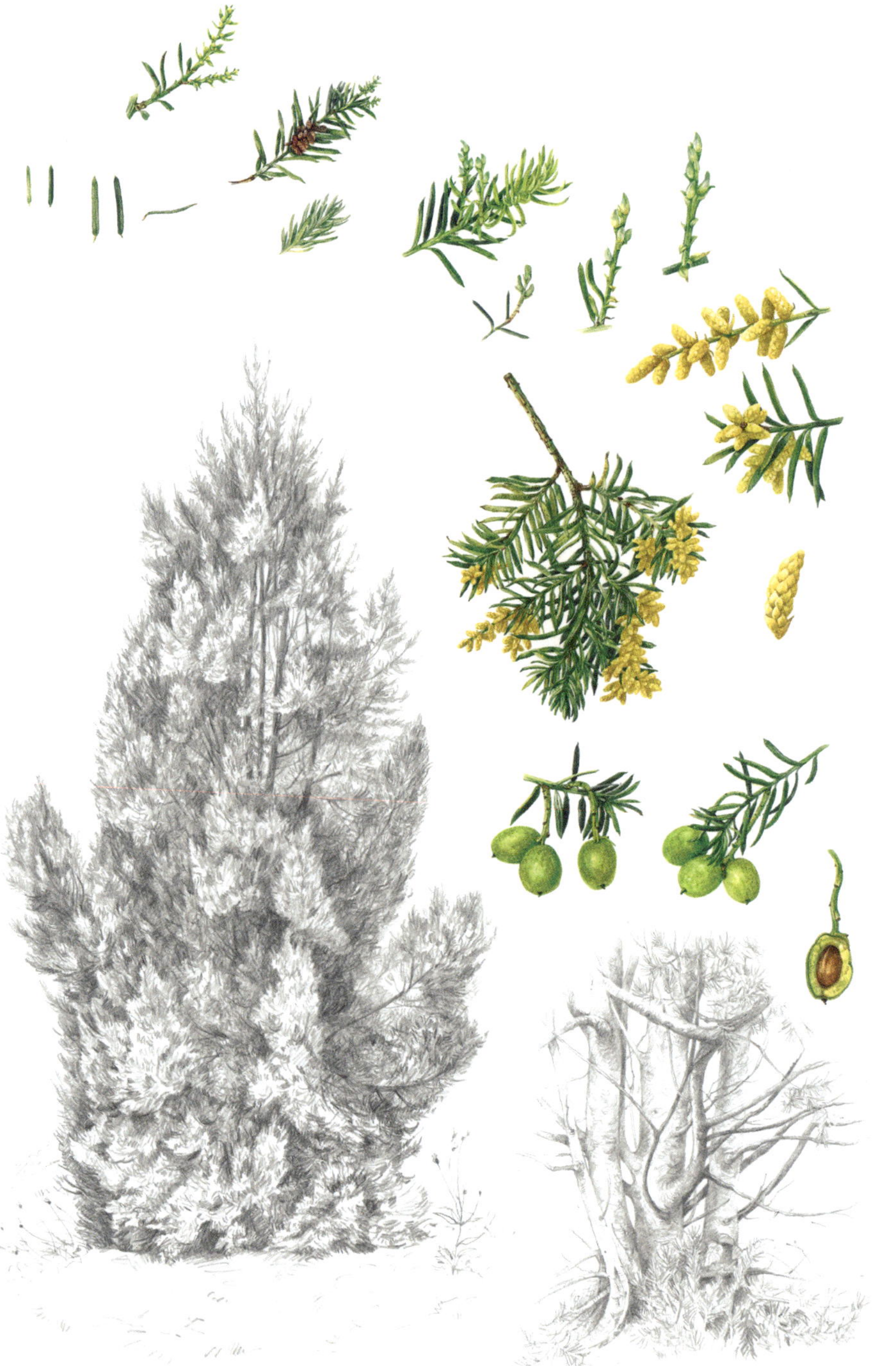

Prumnopitys andina
Chilean plum yew

This tree's seeds need coaxing to germinate. Bedgebury National Pinetum worked with Forest Research and the Royal Botanic Garden Edinburgh to discover the perfect conditions and help to save this threatened conifer.

Sandra Fernandez, 2024
Watercolour and graphite pencil
on watercolour paper

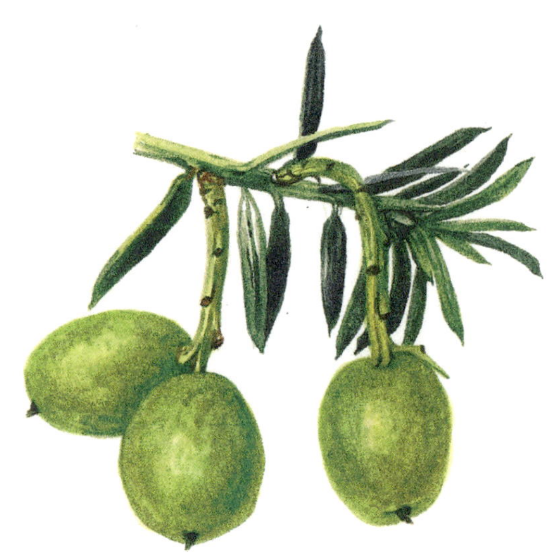

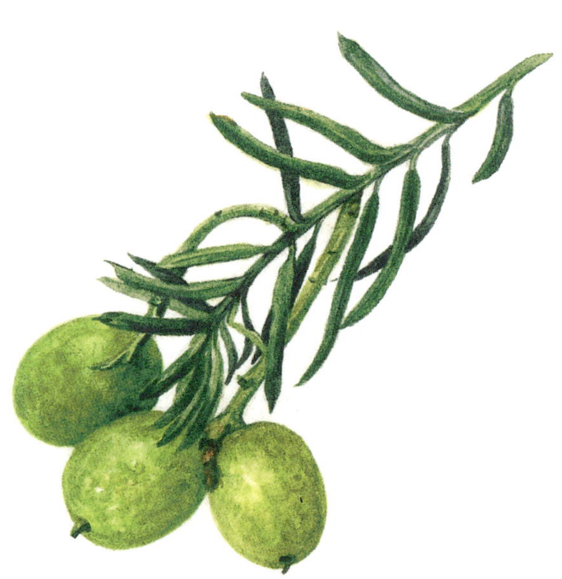

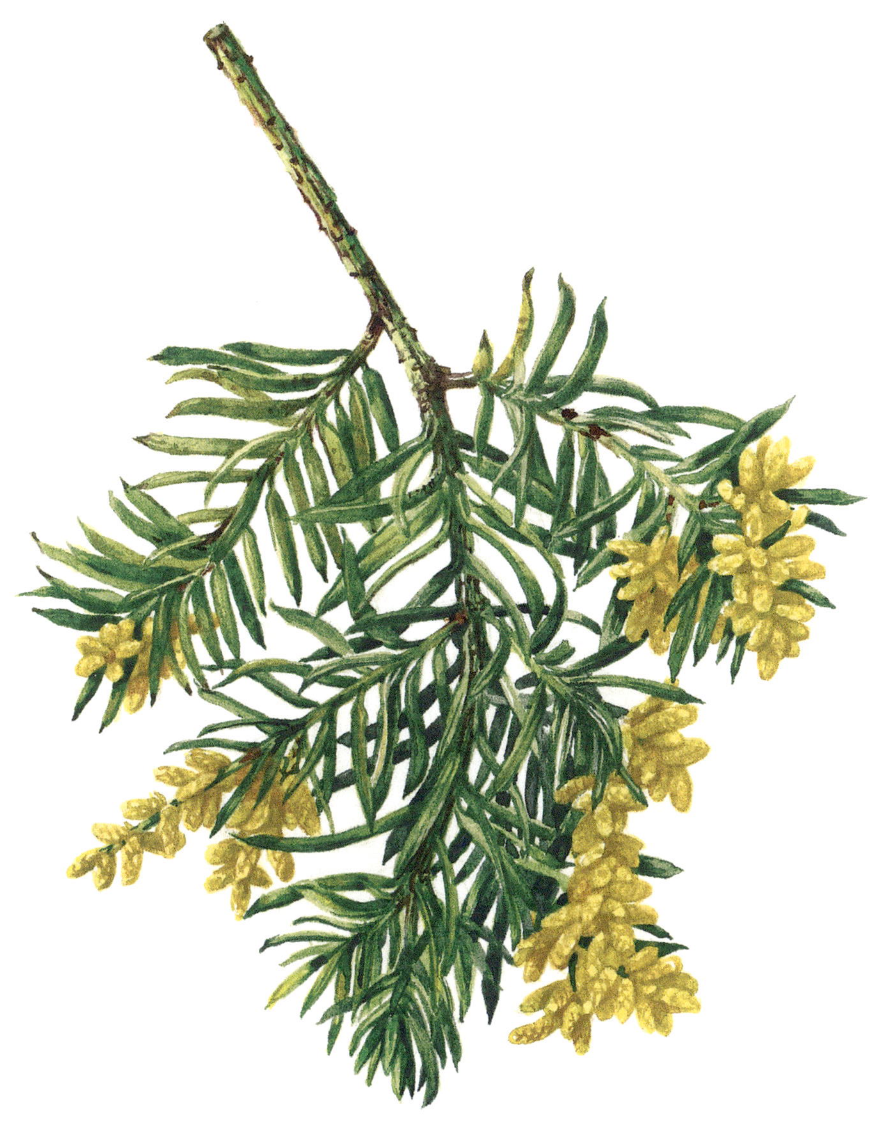

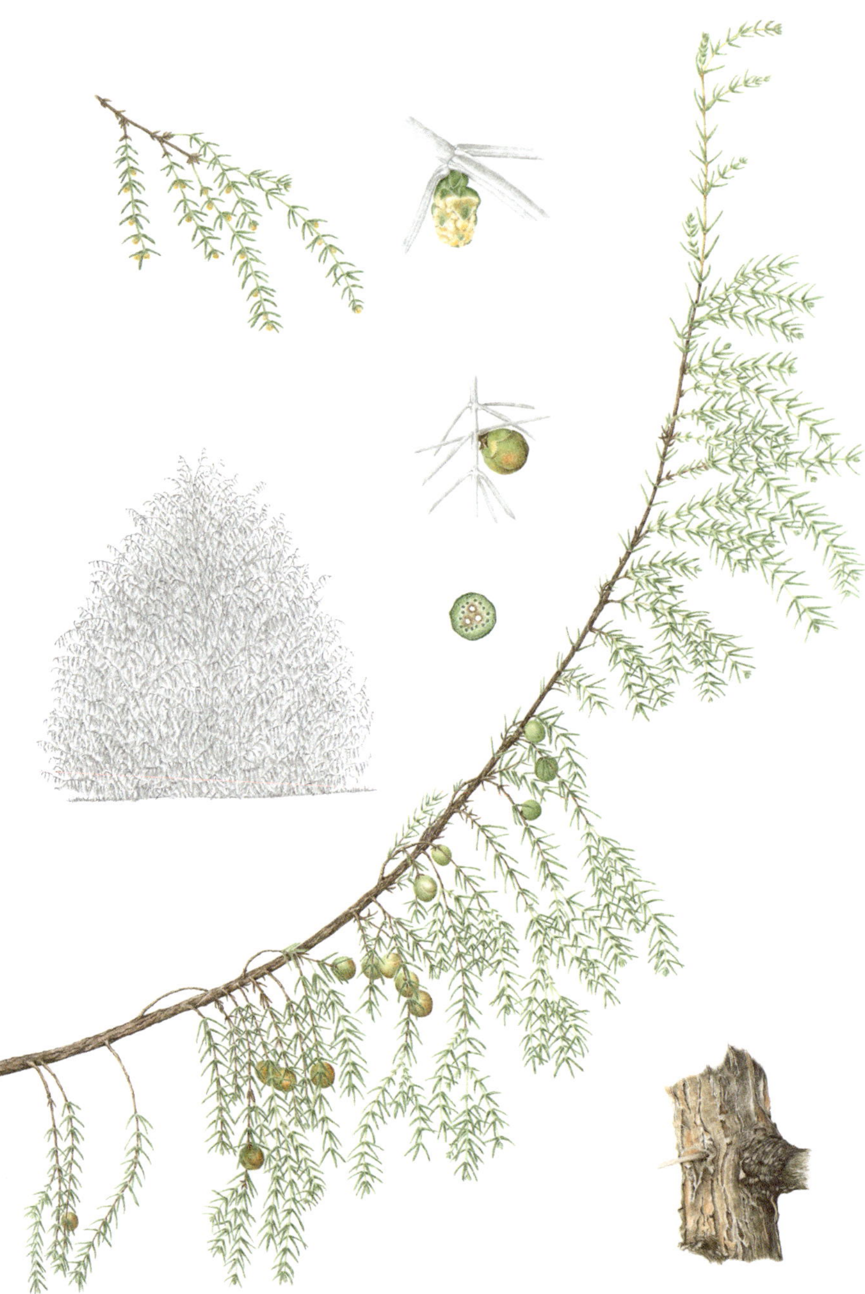

Juniperus cedrus
Canary Island juniper
This tree is endangered in the wild due to felling and predation by wild goats. Coming from warmer conditions, it's an example of how climate change is affecting what can be successfully grown outdoors at Bedgebury.

Helen Cavalli, 2024
Watercolour and graphite pencil on watercolour paper

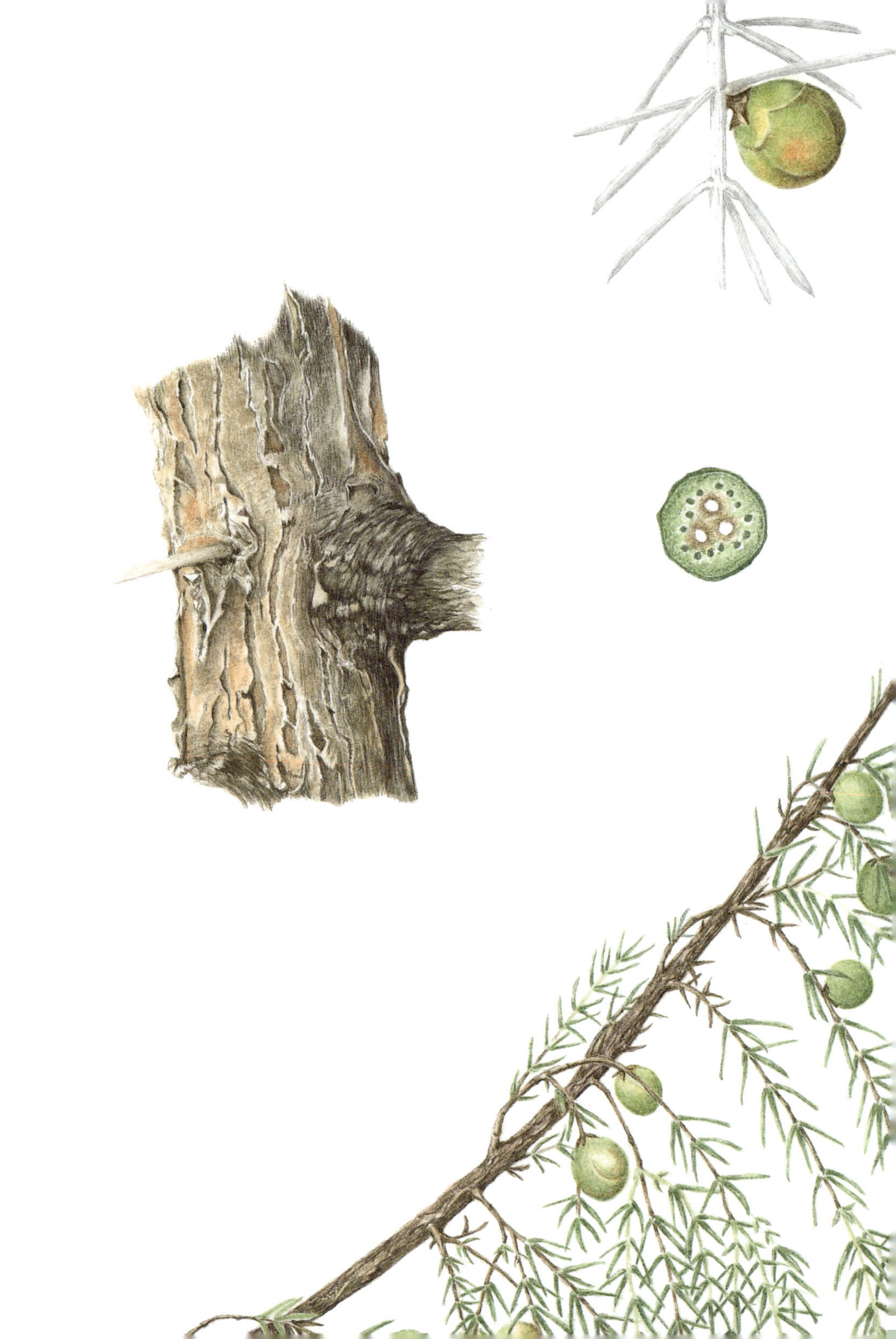

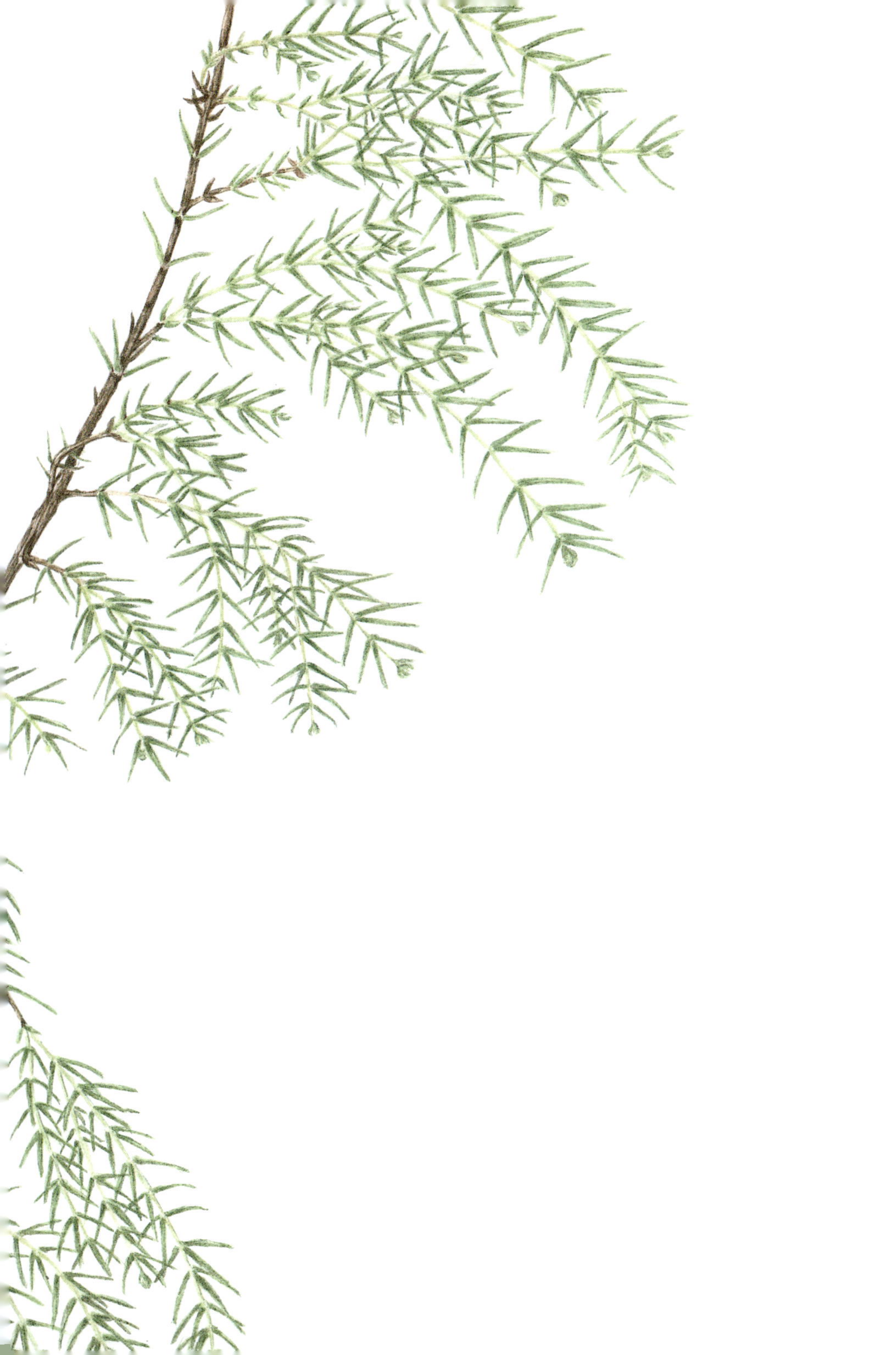

About the artists

The Bedgebury Pinetum Florilegium Society is a group of artists who volunteer their time and skills to create beautiful and botanically accurate paintings and drawings of rare, notable and endangered trees and plants in the Bedgebury National Pinetum.

Louisa Bailey completed a diploma in botanical art with the Society of Botanical Artists in 2012 achieving a distinction. She became a member of Bedgebury National Pinetum Florilegium in 2016 and her works are part of the Pinetum's collection.

Pearl Bostock is the founder Member and Chair of The Bedgebury Pinetum Florilegium Society. She initially trained in Fine Art and gained a Diploma from The English Gardening School at the Chelsea Physic Garden in 2007. Her work is held in private collections throughout the world, and she is an Associate member of the Hampton Court Palace Florilegium Society.

Margaret Brooker has been a member of The Bedgebury Pinetum Florilegium Society since 2010. She has two RHS Silver-Gilt (Lindley) awards and has been a Member of the Society of Botanical Artists. After solo projects, she co-tutored a group at Brogdale National Orchards, qualifying to teach in 2009. She also belongs to a sight loss group for practising artists.

Helen Cavalli trained as a cartographer and has a diploma from the Society of Botanical Artists. She is a Member of the Association of Botanical Artists and Hampton Court Palace Florilegium, where she has five paintings in the archive. Helen's illustrations are featured at the National Botanic Garden of Wales and have also been used in a botanical handbook for artists.

Susan Conroy is a former primary school teacher. She has a diploma from the English gardening school at the Chelsea Physic Garden. She is a founder and fellow member of the Hampton Court Palace Florilegium society, of which she is chairperson. She is the secretary of the Bedgebury National Pinetum's Florilegium Society. She has paintings in the Hampton Court and Bedgebury collections and various private collections.

Jackie Copeman has a diploma from the English Gardening School at Chelsea Physic Garden and has been a member of The Bedgebury Pinetum Florilegium Society since 2014. She is a founder member and now associate member of the Hampton Court Palace Florilegium Society and has painted numerous botanical works from the historic Queen Mary II exotics collection held in the Palace archive.

Sandra Fernandez trained as an illustrator at Harrow College of Art and has an MA in Natural History Illustration from the Royal College of Art. She worked for the London Zoo Design Unit as a freelance illustrator and her work has been exhibited widely including at The Society of Wildlife Artists, The Society of Botanical Artists and the Mall Galleries.

Helen Hiorns completed her diploma from The English Gardening School at the Chelsea Physic Garden in 2010. Soon after she became a member of The Bedgebury Pinetum Florilegium Society. Her work has been shown at Artichoke Gallery Ticehurst, Godalming Museum and Watts Gallery.

Julie Spyropoulos has a degree in Fine Art and a diploma from the English Gardening School at Chelsea Physic Garden. She has painted for the Hampton Court Palace Florilegium Society and for The Bedgebury Pinetum Florilegium Society.

About the authors

Christina Harrison (Hourigan) is an author and garden historian. She is currently completing an AHRC techne-funded PhD with Royal Holloway, University of London and the Royal Botanic Gardens, Kew researching the cultural history of Kew's arboretum and its tree collections. Prior to this she worked at Kew for 21 years in interpretation and publishing. She is the author of *Kew's Big Trees* (Kew Publishing, 2019) and *The Botanical Adventures of Joseph Banks* (Kew Publishing, 2020), and co-author of *Remarkable Trees* (Thames & Hudson and Kew, 2nd edition 2024), *Treasured Trees* (Kew Publishing, 2025) and *Bizarre Botany* (Kew Publishing, 2016), and the forthcoming *Among the Giants: a year at the Kew Arboretum* (Octopus and Kew, 2025).

Dan Luscombe is Collections Manager at Bedgebury National Pinetum, where he has worked for 25 years. He has a National Trust Horticulture Apprenticeship and HND in Horticulture. Dan's passion for trees has taken him around the world, working with partners to protect and conserve rare and endangered species.

Recommended reading

Dallimore, W. (1946). The National Pinetum, Bedgebury, Kent 1925–1945. *Quarterly Journal of Forestry.*

Forestry Commission (2010). *Bedgebury National Pinetum.* Forestry Commission.

Harrison, C. & Kirkham, T. (2024). *Remarkable Trees.* 2nd edition. Thames & Hudson and Kew.

HMSO (1955). *Guide to the National Pinetum and Forest Plots at Bedgebury.* 2nd edition. HMSO, London.

Mitchell, A. F. & Westall, A. W. (eds.) (1972). *Bedgebury Pinetum and Forest Plots.* HMSO, London.

Websites
Bedgebury National Pinetum and Forest
www.forestryengland.uk/bedgebury

International Conifer Conservation Programme
www.rbge.org.uk/science-and-conservation/genetics-and-conservation/conifer-conservation/

Royal Botanic Gardens, Kew
www.kew.org